MY LIFE AS A SAILOR

My Life as a Sailor

Fran Yearly

Writers Club Press
San Jose New York Lincoln Shanghai

My Life as a Sailor

Writers Club Press
an imprint of iUniverse.com, Inc.

For information address:
iUniverse.com, Inc.
5220 S 16th, Ste. 200
Lincoln, NE 68512
www.iuniverse.com

ISBN: 0-595-17510-4

Printed in the United States of America

In memory of Louise Yearly
A dedicated and loving mother in time of war who had the foresight to save her son's diary and letters. Although the pages are now yellow and brittle, they have become a valuable gateway into our country's past.

Foreword

When I was young I remember my father telling me stories about World War II. I was never very interested. It was something I had not experienced and it didn't seem very important to me. One year he took me to the Philadelphia Navy Yard for an open house. As the ferry crossed the Delaware River it passed under an aircraft carrier. I had never seen anything so intimidating. We spent the day walking around the grounds and went aboard a destroyer called the Barton. He told me this was the ship he spent the most time on during the war. Once more, I was not impressed. That night he told my mother that a sailor he was talking to on the Barton was fascinated that my father had served on the ship in World War II. I couldn't understand why.

Time passed by. My father died a relatively young man at the age of 50 in 1976. I moved away from the home and area I grew up in a few years after that. About ten years ago my mother gave me my father's war diary and the 160 letters he wrote home to his parents. Although I was now more appreciative of his military service I never seemed to have the time to sit down and read much of what he had written.

I followed with interest the 50th anniversary commemoration of the D-Day invasion as it received a significant amount of press coverage. I got out my father's diary to see where he was on June 6, 1944 and was stunned to learn that his ship was just a few hundred yards off the coast of Normandy that morning. He had been an eyewitness and active participant in what is universally recognized as one of the defining moments in the history of civilization.

In the months ahead I began to read more of his diary and sift through his many letters. The more I read the more I realized how easy it is to forget our past and the sacrifices that were made for the future. The average age of an American soldier in World War II was around 25. My father enlisted at 17, he was just a kid. In the back of his diary, to this day, is the small branch of a Christmas tree he placed there almost 60 years ago. It was mailed to him during the holidays by his mother while he was on the Barton in the Philippines. In war, it served as a reminder of the life he had left and longed to return to.

Today is the 75th anniversary of my father's birth. A noted historian once said we will never be able to do enough to show our appreciation for the sacrifices that were made so long ago in that war. With the dawn of a new millennium, the dark days of the last century are now shed in a new light. Just like the millions of American soldiers he fought with in World War II, my father will no longer be remembered as an ordinary person. In my eyes he has become a true hero and a legend.

Patrick Francis Yearly
Chantilly, Virginia
March 28, 2000

Introduction

The diary and letters have been combined on the same pages of this book to offer an easy method of following the chronological events of Fran Yearly's service in the Navy. All diary entries are in bold and italicized. The diary was recorded in an 8 by 5 inch pea green canvas backed book. **All entries were recorded the day they happened.** There are no recollections or reminiscences. The only changes I have made were to correct grammar and punctuation. You will notice after January 12, 1945 there are only a few remaining diary entries. My theory is that the diary was discovered by an officer and Fran was reminded that recording events aboard ship was a breach of security.

The letters were sent to Fran's parents who lived on Lippincott Avenue in Riverside. His mother saved every letter and postcard sent during his war years. All letters were signed, "Your Sailor Son and Brother, Fran". I have left this off to avoid repetition.

A copy of this book has been accepted into the permanent collection of the following libraries.

The Library of Congress
Washington, DC

The National D-Day Museum
New Orleans, Louisiana

The Navy Memorial Foundation
Washington, DC

Riverside High School
Riverside, New Jersey

Naval Historical Center
Washington, DC

Joyner Library
Special Collections/Navy Manuscripts
East Carolina University
Greenville, North Carolina

The original diary, all original letters, postcards and scrapbooks will be donated, at a date to be determined, to the National D-Day Museum. They will be kept in permanent storage for availability to historians of the future.

1942

August 24–Enlisted in the U.S. Navy at the Customs House in Philadelphia, Pa.

October 5–Sworn in at Philadelphia and left for the Great Lakes Naval Training Station in Illinois.

October 7–Arrived at "Boot Camp" and assigned to Camp Green Bay. Fellows in the Company were Tom Stewart from Newtown Square, Pa. and Ted Tedesco from Mount Holly, NJ. After boat training, came home on a 9 day leave, then returned to Great Lakes.

October 12, 1942
Great Lakes, Ill.

Dear Folks,

Well today we started our first week of training. The training period doesn't start until we are given our first needles and we received our first one's today. We got two needles and a vaccination. We still have to get a few more. We do not know how long our training is going to be. It will be either 4 or 5 weeks and we will graduate about the 7th of November and then we will have nine days leave. Yesterday, I did my first washing. Boy! Ma, you should have seen us fellows scrubbing, we looked like a bunch of bachelors. You should be here to see us clean the barracks. We have to do this in the morning as soon as we wash up. First we have to sandpaper the floor, steel wool it, sweep it out, wax the floors and then wash the windows.

After this we have to fold our blankets a certain way and put our pillows and towels on the bed. In front of our bunks are posts on which we hang our sea bags which contain our clothes and our ditty bags, which contain our toilet articles. We haven't had our hair cuts yet, but are scheduled to get them tomorrow. When the fellows who have them pass us and see us with our long hair they call us "barber bait".

We really have a swell bunch of fellows in our company and a swell commander. There are a bunch of Irishmen linked together and some really have Irish names such as O'Neill, O'Malley and Murphy. We all chipped in a quarter and bought a radio for our barracks. We can buy anything we want at the Canteen for half price. I miss the Philadelphia papers for we only get the papers from Chicago here. The food is really good, but I sure miss those you make Ma. We have plenty to eat and a different kind of meat every meal, but the coffee is awful.

The gymnasiums are almost as big as Lakehurst hanger. Most of the fellows in my company are from Pennsylvania, but there are fellows here from Camden, Medford, Moorestown and Beverly. I met Mary Clauss' boyfriend's brother on Saturday. He's from Riverside and has been here two weeks. Well I'll close for now hoping to hear from you soon. Love to all.

October 12, 1942
Postcard of USS Brooklyn

Dear Butz,

How would you like to sail this in a mud puddle? I'll bet it would take you a couple of years to clean this ship.

October 15, 1942
Great Lakes, Ill.

Dear Folks,

Well here I am again. I received your letter this morning, the first mail I have had so far. I wrote you a letter and a postal card. I guess you'll have them by the time you receive this letter. Tell the Dietrichs and the Hartmans to write. Also, tell Skin to write and let me know how the team is doing.

I'm really glad I had a chance to enlist and get in the Navy. The Chicago papers are full of big headlines where the President asks for 1,500,000 men and the drafting of fellows 18 to 19. There are at least ten fellows in my company who are 17. There are a couple of fellows about the size of Vince.

After one week I eat like a house at every meal. Things like carrots, sweet potatoes, liver and pepper salad that I wouldn't touch at home I eat with vigor now. Yesterday we were taught how to roll our clothes and put them in the sea bag. In the afternoon we drilled for about two hours and then went to the bunkers.Boy! folks you should see us now. We look like a bunch of convicts with our haircuts and blue denims. That's about the fastest haircut I ever had in 40 seconds. They move out of that chair like an assembly line. It started to rain last night and has been drizzling all day. Today we had a big inspection. We had to roll all our clothes and lay them out on our bunks. We were inspected by a lieutenant and a chief petty officer. Because of the rain that's all we had to do. We have from 4:30 to 9:30 to ourselves every night, but when the time comes and you want to write alot of letters we find that we have washing to do and before you realize it half the night's gone.

I'll be glad when we change from our whites to our blues. Tell Vince to get those chickens on the hustle so he can make some money for himself. How's Paul doing in school, is he still car washing? Tell Dad not to work so hard. Well it's getting late now and time to go to bed so I'll close with loads of love to all.

P.S. Enclosed is a receipt for my clothes sent home.

October 17, 1942
Great Lakes, Ill.

Dear Folks,

Just a few more lines to let you know how I'm doing. Well we've been in training a week tomorrow and so far our company has been really doing good. I felt really good today because I received six letters. I guess I hit the jackpot. I got a letter from the Dietrichs and from Johnny Wilhelm and some other of my school pals that I wrote to. Yesterday I received a letter from Bubbles Bachmann. Her brother is at the same place as John is, only in a different service. They are going down to see him on the 28th.

Yesterday was field day. By this I mean house cleaning, not marching. We cleaned out the barracks all day yesterday and this morning. Today we had Captain's inspection. There were about 2,000 sailors all lined up in their white uniforms. The Chief commended us on having such a clean barracks and we were allowed to listen to the football games this afternoon for having such a good inspection.

I'm beginning to feel strong and healthy now with this early morning exercise and I eat 3 full square meals a day. I feel like I gained five pounds already. I'm doing all right so don't worry about me. I know about almost everybody in my company now and they're a bunch of swell fellows. They have an "Empty Bottle Quartet" here and sing songs while we clean out the barracks. There are alot of comedians too.

In the letter I got from Dot Dietrich she said that Vince was at the dance Saturday night and that he's running for President of his class. Boy! he's really getting along fast. Tell him to keep it up and really study. How's Butz making out with his scrap drive? Well I have to close now so with loads of love to all.

October 22, 1942
Great Lakes, Illinois

Dear Folks,

Just to let you know that I have received all of your letters and papers that you sent me. The fellows were glad to read a Philadelphia paper. Boy! the October weather is really with us now. The beginning of the week we had a two day rain, then the next day the sun was out. Yesterday it was really cold. Today we had a northeaster and when we went to morning chow it was raining cats and dogs. It cleared up in the middle of the day, but we still had to wear lots of clothes and even our woolen gloves. I guess we will be out of here before the heavy snows, although this morning it snowed a little. I guess you are still having good old Jersey weather. It's all right to do this, talking about the weather, because our mail is not censored.

I have been kept pretty busy this week. The day before yesterday we marched to a camp about 2 miles away to attend an insurance lecture and take out an insurance policy. The next day we marched to the same place for another lecture on allotments for our dependents. We drill about two hours in the morning and about three in the afternoon. Sometimes we think we are in the army. Yesterday we were given our "dog tags" and today we got our identification pictures. Tomorrow we are to get our 4th and 5th shots. These are to be the double typhoid. I did not get sick from the first three, but it makes your arm mighty sore and I had a puffed out arm from the vaccination.

We are already making plans for coming home. We have filled out our railroad ticket slips, our home address location and we are counting the days and weeks until we get our leave. We graduate on the 7th and leave on the 7th. We have to be back by noon on the 16th. We will not get any weekend leave into Chicago as we are only to get four weeks of training. Next week I think our company will go on KP for the week, the rest will go on guard duty.

I am up to my neck in mail now. I received 15 letters in the last four days. Bernie wrote to me and all through his letter he said nothing but how surprised he was. He said that he wished he was out of school so that he could join me. I have written to everyone that I could think of and I have heard from almost everyone. What's the matter with the Hartmans? There was a second letter I wrote when I got here and I've been here two weeks now and didn't hear from anyone of them at this writing. If you see Skin, Doris or Louise tell them to write because I would like to hear from them.

Last night I did an hour and a half's washing. We have to have all our whites clean for Saturday's inspection. I'll be glad when we put them away for the winter and start wearing our blues, then we won't have so much washing to do. I sent the sisters a card and they wrote me a letter thanking me and sent a holy picture and a medal.

I was on guard duty from 12 to 4 PM yesterday. We do not guard outside, but inside of the barracks. There is a front door guard, a washroom guard, and the dormitory guard. Well, it's 9:25 now and I have to hop in bed before the lights go out. We will be pretty busy tomorrow again because it is field day and time to clean the barracks. Tell Vince I will answer his letter when I get time. Give my love to all and tell Dad to take it easy in work because we will win the war.

October 27, 1942
Great Lakes, Ill.

Dear Folks,

I received Ma and Dad's letters and the package on Sunday. I sure enjoyed the package alot and so did the fellows. The candy, cookies and fruit lasted exactly one day. It sure was good and I shared it with the fellows who hung around me. Lots of fellows are receiving packages now. Our company gets the most mail of the whole battalion. We get 4 and 5 packs each time it is given out. We get mail twice a day and once on Sunday.

I am doing fine and did not receive the slightest effects from the needles we got just that my arm was a little sore. We are now counting the days and meals until we leave. One fellow said we just have 30 more meals here (Thank God). We get good things to eat, but not enough of it. I can't wait until we get our furlough so I can feast on your good cooking Ma. Boy! that fried chicken and mashed potatoes with gravy, mmmmm!

I was on fire guard yesterday from 4PM to 8PM. We had to patrol among the barracks with a guard belt and a club. We inspect the boiler room and look out for fires among the barracks. It still is pretty cold up here. The wind is really blowing and it "stings" your face. The lowest temperature so far was 22 degrees at 8AM yesterday. I hope we leave before we really get a good snowfall. They say it gets to 30 below in winter.

Today is Navy Day and almost all the programs on the radio were about the Navy. The Chicago papers were full of it and there were supposed to be three Admirals in Chicago to review a parade. I am writing this letter in a hurry tonight as it's 9PM and I just got through washing and taking a shower. I am going to write to the Hartmans again tomorrow for maybe they did not receive my first letter. So far I still have not heard from them. Well I'll close now as it's 9:20 and time to climb into bed. Give my love to all.

November 15, 1942
Chicago, Ill.

Dear Folks,

We arrived safely here in Chicago (Union Station) at 6PM (our time). We managed to find some seats up near the engine in back of the baggage car. When we reached Altoona, Pa. there were several inches of snow on the ground and all the way into Chicago it was the same way. The weather was about the same everywhere. It is pretty warm now.

Boy! that train was sure crowded. Mostly sailors and soldiers were on it. After we arrived in Chicago we came here to the U.S.O. and took a hot shower. We were really black and dirty from the trip. We checked in our things and we are sleeping here for the night and catching an early train to the Great Lakes in the morning. We just came in from "sight seeing" on the town. Chicago really is a large town. Everywhere there are sailors and soldiers. Well I guess that's all the news for now so I'll close for the present. Love to you all.

P.S. Do not write to this address as it's still my old one.

November 17, 1942
Great Lakes, Ill.

Dear Folks,

We arrived at the Main Station at 7:30AM on Monday and reported right away. They took our leave papers and we were assigned to a barracks. We five fellows were split up as some of us are going to seaman's school and the others to trade school. You should see this barracks. It's a big hangar-like barracks and there are 2,000 men and we now sleep in triple-deck bunks. Since Monday morning we don't have anything to do but sit on our bunks and read and sleep. This building is used for nothing but sleeping here until the men are transported to school. Then a group of men is called out to leave (this is known as a "draft" of men). Our "draft" was called today and we think we will leave tomorrow morning (Wednesday). We don't know where we're going for sure, but we know of either two places where we will be sent, but we are not allowed to write about it. It is two states in the U.S. I think the 2000 of us will leave tomorrow. I met "Ott" Daniels and we are bunked near each other and trying to stick together so that maybe we will be sent to the same place. Our chief gave us a lecture yesterday and told us that we shouldn't be discouraged because we didn't make school. He has been in the Navy 25 years and most of his time was spent at sea.

He never went to trade school, but went to sea. He said that with our learning from the "old timers" out in the fleet by experience we would have a rating quicker than those people going to school and learning from books. He said you'll never win a war in school. Whichever state we go to we will go to school for a few months and then go to sea. If it was up to us fellows we would just as leave go out on a ship right now. You should see our chow line. Whew! before it was 200 men in line, now it's 2000. This is really a swell camp. There are white shingled barracks and green grass and sidewalks. The Great Lakes broadcasting station is only about two blocks from here as we can see the high tower. They have tailor shops, a laundry, movies, swimming pools, a post office, canteens and a modernistic restaurant for servicemen.

Just across from our "chow house" is where the prisoners are stationed. There are 500 of them and they are in two barracks surrounded by a bob wire fence about 10 feet high. There are Marine guards around the place with tommy guns and high powered rifles. When they march them across the street to "chow" they rope off the whole street and they have to march across with their arms folded. They are made to wear blue dungarees and all over the dungarees are painted big P's with white paint.

Well this is a mighty long letter and I've run out of things to write about. I'll drop you cards with the progress of our train trip. Until then, I remain with loads of love to all.

P.S. Where are Lawrence Yearly and George Banyas at?

November–Transferred from Great Lakes to the Receiving Barracks in Brooklyn, NY. Stayed there until December 12.

December 1, 1942
Postcard
New York City

Dear Folks,
Arrived here at the barracks OK about 3:15 AM. I went to the dentist today and had two teeth filled. I got a letter from John and Al. I don't know if I can see Al as he is in quarantine. John is disgusted because he will not be able to get leave for at least 7 months. He said he is due to start school in February.

December 2, 1942
Brooklyn, N.Y.

Dear Folks,
Well folks I'm still here yet and haven't heard anything about our ship being in. This week is really flying along. Here it is Wednesday already. We have only to wait tomorrow and Friday morning and then we will be sure to be home for the weekend. They don't give you much notice as about 10 of the fellows in this barracks were notified and were

out of here in about an hour. However, I think that we will make this weekend home.

I received a letter from the Haners and said something about they and the Horners coming over here on Sunday. But I wrote them right away and told them I expect to go home this weekend. This is really a small world. Last night I met another fellow from Riverside. The fellow who lives on Webster Street. His name is Givonetti. He was shipped here from Newport. I ran into him down at the canteen. Boy! were we surprised to meet each other. We saw a Broadway show that played here last night. It was really good and was put on by the U.S.O. Camp Shows. Well I guess that's all for now so I'll close.

December 9, 1942
Brooklyn, New York

I arrived at the station on Monday morning at 4AM. I came in on the 1:18 as far as New York with Jack Yoest. I guess you thought that I shipped out because you didn't hear from me before this. But it was declared a general field day on Monday. And did we work as this was for the admiral's inspection. We had to scrub our hammocks and seabags, sweep up, wash windows, swab the deck etc. This place was like a bee hive. We had to stand inspection in our dress blues and I never saw so many gold braids in all my life. Lieutenants, Commanders, Captains and Ensigns were with the Admiral. He was loaded with gold braids. We passed his inspection okay so we had some liberty Monday night. I took the opportunity to go over to the Howes. I went as far as Newark with a fellow from my barracks. We took the Hudson tube into Newark and then I took a bus to Irvington. I didn't have any trouble at all getting there even though it was dark. I arrived at a quarter to seven. Boy! were they surprised to see me. Dot called up the Howes right away and they came over about 10. I took the 1:15 bus from their place and I got here at 3AM. So between Monday and Tuesday night I had about 7 hours sleep and I slept all day yesterday and went to be early last night to make up for it. So today was the first chance I had to write.

It started snowing early this morning and just stopped about an hour ago. There are a couple inches on the ground. Last night a program was broadcast over CBS. The fellows sang songs. Maybe you heard it. It started at 5 o'clock. Last night I also saw Pat O'Brien and Jackie Cooper in "The Navy Comes Through". It was swell. Tonight we are going to see another movie and a U.S.O. show. Also, Frank Sinatra is going to be here in person. He's appearing at the Paramount Theater in New York.

I had a letter from John and he was pretty happy as he said that he may be able to come home sometime around Christmas. I hope that I can get home then too. There is some talk around that we may be here for at least a few weeks yet. I hope so. We're still not doing nothing much. I had liberty last night too, but I stayed in and got some sleep instead of going out. Well I'll close now and I hope that you're better and up and around now Ma. I'm saying a prayer for you.

December 11, 1942
Brooklyn, New York

Dear Folks,

I've just talked with Ma on the phone and I'm now in the auditorium writing this letter. Almost all of the fellows are being transferred out today. Some are going to Boston, some to Long Island and a bunch of us are going to Casco Bay–Portland, Maine. We heard that our ship is up there and whether we will leave or be around for a few weeks we do not know as yet. We are to leave some time this afternoon. I'll write when I arrive there. I am sending a list of people to send cards to, if they do not arrive in time maybe you could send some ordinary cards.

Well, that's all for now so I'll close. I'll try and drop you a line and let you know about our trip. Give my love to all and God bless you all.

December 12–Transferred from the Receiving Barracks in Brooklyn to Casco Bay in Portland, Maine.

December 13, 1942
Casco Bay
Portland, Maine

Dear Folks,

I arrived here safely and I'm now at the receiving barracks. As we're under naval censorship I won't be able to say much or describe our surroundings. It's about three times as cold as it was at the Great Lakes. It has been snowing since this morning and the snow looks beautiful lying on the pine and birch bark trees.

We have swell food here. Three good ones a day. For Sunday dinner we had roast chicken, mashed potatoes and gravy, string beans, cauliflower, salad dressing, bread and butter, cake, ice cream and coffee. What a meal! We also have recreation with bowling alleys, ping-pong and pool tables, a canteen, movies, gyms and soda foutains.

I don't know if we'll get home for Christmas or not. If the Christmas cards come, Vince can send them out. Send me one so I can see what they look like. Also, try and send me the Press as I would like to hear some news. I could use a few dollars too Ma, I'm getting pretty low as I spent $8.20 worth on clothes. Am I glad too because I bought some winter underwear. I sure can use them. Tell Hank Mitsch and Skin that I was asking about them. I'll close for now and hope that everyone is well at home. Give everyone my love and may God bless you all.

December 16—Transferred from Casco Bay, Maine to Pier 92 in New York City for further transfer to the destroyer USS Simpson (221).

December 18–Transferred to the destroyer Simpson and assigned to the Deck Force.

December 24–Left New York with a convoy to Key West, Florida (was seasick for two days).

December 31–Arrived with the convoy at Key West (went from Deck Force to the Fireroom as a Tender Third Class on December 27).

1943

January 1–Left Key West and returned to New York City (made two trips to Key West).

USS Simpson
January 11, 1943

Dear Folks,

I arrived here safely about 4:30 AM this morning. I did not have any difficulty getting here as I made good connections on both the subway and the ferry. I slept on the train coming up and still got a few hours sleep after I arrived on the ship. I didn't have much to do today except to "turn too" after chow and help clean up the fire rooms a little. There is supposed to be an inspection of the ship sometime this week and we think that after this our leave may start. I sure hope so.

I am writing this letter before the movies start. They are going to show "Union Pacific". It's a story about the founding of the Union Pacific railroad. Well I guess that's all that I can write about just now so I'll close hoping that we get leave and that I'll be seeing you soon.

P. S.–I had a letter from Nilhelens and he is stationed in South Carolina. He say's it's not so "hot" down there and he doesn't expect to get any leave until Easter.

January 18, 1943
Postcard
Key West

Dear Folks,

I am feeling fine and am all right. We spent our Christmas at sea, but we had a big feast. I was sea sick for two days, but I am used to it now and I'm an "old salt". Has John been home lately? Maybe I'll get to see him while he's home.

USS Simpson
January 18, 1943

Dear Folks,

I got the 1:18 train out of Philadelphia and arrived in Penn Station at 3 o'clock. I made good connections on both the subway and ferry. I arrived here at the ship about 4:30 and still got a few hours sleep before reveille. We "turned too" today and cleaned out the inside of the boiler. It's now 7:30 PM and I'm writing this while I'm waiting for the movies to start. There's a fellow playing an accordion and we just sent a fellow down to the canteen for some ice cream so I guess it's just like being ashore. The movie is going to be one of the "Blondie" movies. I have the 12 to 4 watch tonight so right after the movies I'll have to go on duty. I'll be seeing you on Wednesday if we get 1 o'clock liberty. Until then I'll have to close for now as the movies are about to start. Closing with love to you all I remain, as always, your loving sailor son.

January 29, 1943
Postcard
Key West, Florida

Hi Folks,

Enjoying the Florida sunshine. It's really hot down here. I'll bet you're freezing back home. Be seeing you soon.

February 9, 1943
Postcard
"I'm All out for Victory"

Dear Folks,

Arrived here at the ship safely about 4AM. I just came in off watch. I had the 4 to 8 on the deck. I just passed some of my candy out to the fellows and it vanished in a few seconds. It was really cold here today, maybe Pete and Skin will get in some more ice skating.

February 9, 1943

Dear Folks,

I'm writing this letter from the USO club in Thompkinsville. I just came from a tailor shop where I had my suit pressed, got a shoe shine and had something to eat. I stayed in to write a few letters and then I'm going to the movies down the street to see "Black Swan".

I got back at 4AM on Monday morning, unpacked and had a couple hours sleep before reveille. It's pretty cold now. The latest I heard is that we going to be here until Thursday, then we're going into the Yard for a few days. I hope that maybe I will get a chance to get home again. Well I'll close for now. Give my love to all.

USS Simpson
February 13, 1943

Dear Folks,

I arrived at the ship about 3 AM because of the holidays. I suppose they had more trains on for I caught the 12:27 out of 30th Street station and got here on the ship early. I guess you were pretty excited when you found out I forgot my wallet. Talk about confusion. Just as the Philadelphia bus pulled up, Harris came over to Dad and said something about a wallet. Dad had to hand me some money quick just as the bus pulled out. It's a good thing he gave me some as I had my return ticket in my wallet and had to buy another round trip ticket. We got paid today so I won't be too short.

I had to stand the 8 to 12 watch on the dock this morning and it was pretty nasty as it snowed all morning. That sure was a swell package of goodies you made up for me Ma, I'm pretty well stocked up on eats now. My locker looks like the ship canteen. I shared some of the things with the fellows and they enjoyed it alot. I received your letter today and it had stamped on it "returned for postage" so that explains why I didn't get it last week. I'm glad you sent me that prayer book now as it has some nice prayers in it. If I can't get to mass I can at least read it from the book.

From the way things look it seems we are going on a long trip and will be gone for some time. I think that maybe we will see some action. I'm not afraid as I just went to confession and communion last week and I'm praying to St. Christopher for my safe return. Don't worry about me and lets hope with God's will that I'll be home real soon again. Love to all.

P.S.–Tell everyone to write me often even though they don't hear from me as I may not have the chance to write so often to them.

P.S.S.–If you can, try and send me the Press once in a while.

February 14–The Simpson in New York City–We fueled the ship and prepared to get underway.

February 15–Left at 0800. Temperature was below zero. Visibility poor due to steam arising from the water. There was ice on the deck and guns.

February 16–On Tuesday afternoon arrived in Virginia Beach, Va. and dropped anchor.

February 17–Stayed at Virginia Beach all day.

February 18–Hoisted anchor and left Virginia Beach. Picked up a convoy of about 40 ships.

February 19–Getting warmer with nice moonlit nights. Convoy fired today.

February 20–Slightly cloudy. Fired again today.

February 21–Light rain and overcast. Rough sea today. Approximately 1000 miles out.

February 22–Clocks went one hour ahead. Rough sea and rain. We fueled the ship at sea.

February 23–Very rough sea with white caps, high waves and rain (slightly sea sick). Ran into a storm in the afternoon and saw mountainous waves.

February 24–Storm cleared up and the sun came out.

February 25–Overcast with rain showers. We fueled the ship at sea from a tanker.

February 26–Swell day with an almost calm sea. Estimated time zone II clocks put ahead one hour. We're about 1800 miles out. Sighted smoke on the horizon this morning. It turned out to be a Spanish freighter. Another destroyer had sub contact.

February 27–Calm sea. It rained all day and we fueled the ship at sea. The crew was issued battle helmets and gas masks. One of our escorts had contact this morning with a submarine.

February 28–Light rain showers with a calm sea. We are entering time zone III. Clocks set ahead one hour as we get near the Azores.

February 29–Clear and warm.

March 1–Choppy sea. It hailed about five minutes around chow time.

March 2–Calm and warm. We are now entering dangerous waters about 4-5 days out of North Africa. We expect to arrive either Sunday or Monday.

March 3–Warm, blue sky with a calm sea.

March 4–Calm, warm and a blue sky. Lone plane circled the convoy in the morning.

March 5–Calm sea and very warm. We entered time zone IV. Clocks set ahead one hour. Had two sub contacts during the night. Jefferies dropped depth charges. PBY planes coming out to patrol during day.

March 6–Arrived in Casablanca, North Africa about 1330 PM. We patrolled the harbor until after sun down and then dropped anchor.

March 7–Lay at anchor all day. Watched Arabs going by in fishing boats.

March 8–Beautiful day. Very warm. Lifted anchor and entered the harbor in the afternoon. Tied up to the oil docks. Many Arabs were along the dock in shabby clothes.

March 9–Loaded stoves all day. Stood 2000-2400 watch on dock. Tide here drops 15-20 feet in an hour. Sold old mattress covers and old clothes to the Arabs.

March 10 —Left oil dock in the morning, went out to sea and operated with a French sub. Fired 3" guns. Returned to Casablanca in the afternoon and tied up to the dock.

March 11–Left the harbor in the morning and formed a convoy. Believed to be going to Gibraltar.

March 12 —General Quarters held at 0600. Radar contact at 0700. Search lights were thrown on the ship which proved to be an English Corvette. Choppy sea with pouring rain. Reached Gibraltar about 1300. Sighted French and Spanish Morocco. Dropped anchor in the harbor. Liberty declared until 2200. We went ashore in a whale boat and spent an interesting liberty on the "Rock". Obtained some swell souvenirs. Heard that the German boat Von Trippitz was sunk not far from here.

March 13 —Laid in the harbor at Gibraltar all day. Underway after supper.

March 13, 1943
Postcard
Gibraltar

Am all right and feeling fine. Remember me to all.

March 14—Clear day, calm sea. Expect to arrive at Casablanca in the afternoon. Out of New York one month today.

March 14, 1943
Casablanca

Dear Folks,

This is the first chance I have had to write to you. I am well and feeling fine and everything is all right. I can not say much as we are under censorship regulations.The places I have been so far have been very interesting and I am getting many souvenirs.

Tell everyone that I was asking about them and to keep writing. I'll bet the old town is pretty dull now. Save the Press for me so that I'll be able to read the news when I get home. Tell Skin to get his fishing tackle ready because if we get a leave when we get back we'll go up to the lakes and go trout fishing. Also tell him when he goes to the Saturday night dances to cut a couple of rugs for me. Ma, I wish you and Pete a Happy Birthday and eat a big piece of birthday cake for me We can celebrate my birthday when I come home and you can make one of your extra special chocolate fudge cakes for me. Well I'll close for now. Love to all and don't worry about me.

March 15—Clear day and very warm. Went ashore in Casablanca on liberty. Picked up several swell souvenirs.

March 16—Clear day and warm. Tied up in the harbor all day.

March 16, 1943
Casablanca

Dear Folks,

This has been my first chance to write to you and even now I haven't much to say because of censorship regulations. I just want you to know that I am all right and everything is fine. We took a rather long cruise this time and it has been quite an interesting one for me.

I hope all of you are all right and well. Ma and Pete, I wish you both a Happy Birthday and when I get back home we can celebrate all of our birthdays together with one big party. Give my regards to all the people back home and tell them I was asking about them. Tell everyone to keep on writing to me so I'll have a big pile of letters when I get back. I'll close thinking of you all and sending my love.

March 17–Went out to sea and operated with a French sub. We fired our 3 inch guns.

March 18–Stayed in the harbor all day. In the morning a big convoy came in with six transports. There were also two carriers, the New York and Brooklyn, and about 12 destroyers.

March 18, 1943
Postcard
Casablanca

I am well and everything all right. Don't worry.

March 19–Lay at anchor.

March 20–Stayed in the harbor.

March 21–Had patrol duty outside the harbor.

March 22 —Remained in the harbor all day.

March 23–Remained in the harbor all day.

March 24–Patrol duty again.

March 25–Patrol duty again.

March 25, 1943

Dear Folks,

A few lines to let you know that I am all right and feeling fine. I only wish I could be back home now so that we could celebrate our three birthdays together. However, I'm looking forward to one of your delicious cakes when I get back Ma.

I hope that you received my two previous letters and cards that I sent last week. I will continue to drop you a letter whenever I have the chance. How are Pete and Butz making out? Are they still having their daily fights? Tell Pete he better start studying for those June exams. Do

Pete and Skin still have those "Chili Bowl" haircuts? We had a treat last night. We had ice cream for supper and a movie up on topside. Give all the folks back home my regards and tell them I was asking about them. Tell Dad that he shouldn't work so hard. Well I'll close now thinking of you all and sending you my love.

March 26–Layed at anchor while it rained.

March 27–Clear and very warm.

March 28–Slightly cloudy. Today is my 18th birthday. We went ashore in a whale boat and I went to church at the base.

March 29–Went out to sea and operated with a French sub. Very warm.

March 30–Underway in the morning headed for Gibraltar with the convoy.

March 31–Arrived at the harbor of Gibraltar in the morning. Got underway for Casablanca after supper.

April 1–Started mess cooking today (my troubles begin).

April 2–Remained in the harbor all day.

April 2, 1943

Dear Folks,

How are all of you folks back home making out? I am all right and feeling fine. I started mess cooking yesterday and I'll have it for 3 months until July. You should see me washing dishes.

I'll bet it's beginning to get nice back home now. I guess Pete will be chasing the lawn mower around the yard pretty soon. We aren't receiving any mail, but tell everyone to keep writing so I'll have lots of letters waiting for me. I sure would like to know what the news is back home.

I don't know when we will be getting back home, but I sure hope that it will be soon. I am looking forward to some of your good cooking when I get home Ma. Give all the folks my regards, tell them I was asking about them and to keep writing. Tell Skin to leave some trout in the lakes for me so that I'll be able to catch some. I'll bet he's getting his tackle out already for opening day. I bet Pete and Butz are glad that school is about over. Tell Butz that he better be good because the Easter Bunny will be around soon. I'll close for now thinking of you all and sending you my love. Tell Dad not to work so hard and don't worry about me.

April 3–Arrived in Gibraltar and stayed in the harbor all day.

April 4–Underway in the afternoon for Casablanca.

April 5–Returning to Casablanca with the other destroyers.

April 6–Arrived in Casablanca and anchored in the harbor.

April 7–Lay at anchor all day.

April 8—Lay at anchor all day.

April 9–In the harbor all day. Had Ready Duty. Called out at 2400 to investigate sub contact outside the harbor entrance.

April 10–Patrolled off Casablanca all day.

April 11–Picked up the convoy in the morning. 2100–Destroyer on the starboard side of the convoy dropped charges for about half an hour right in the channel.

April 12–Patrolling in position about 10 miles in front of the convoy. Clocks set back one hour.

April 13–Cloudy with a choppy sea.

April 14–Rough weather with a high wind. Broke all the dishes on my mess table.

April 15–Storm is letting up. Sighted a ship on the horizon and went to investigate. Came along the side of a ship. It was a Spanish freighter headed for Lisbon, Portugal. The clocks went back one hour.

April 16–Rough water with a light wind.

April 17–Storm letting up and it's getting calm. Clear moonlit nights.

April 18–(Palm Sunday) Very clear day and warm. Fired 20MM's. Steaming at 13 knots. Because of an evaporator failure we started rationing water. One bucket of water per man a day.

April 19–Clear and warm. We are supposed to get in one week from today. Had submarine contact in the morning and dropped 8 depth charges. Clocks set back one hour.

April 20–Clear and warm. Had contact around 1300. Went to General Quarters (GQ) at 1430. Dropped 23 depth charges on a sub. A large oil slick appeared on the surface.

April 21–Rough water and cloudy. No water for washing. Drinking water only.

April 22–Ran into a gale. High wind and rough weather. Fueled the ship. Clocks were set back one hour. Approximately 600 miles yet to go.

April 23–Still very rough weather. Waves as big as a house. One enormous wave came over the ship, down the hatch, and flooded a compartment with two feet of water. Convoy had to slow to 10 knots.

April 24–Sea calmed down. Blue sky and very warm. Convoy fired. Still no water except for drinking. Convoy increased to 12 knots.

April 25–Easter Sunday–Beautiful day and very warm. About 100 miles out of New York. Sighted smoke on the horizon and went to investigate. Found it to be an old freighter belonging to the Irish Free State.

April 26–Nice weather and warm. Expect to reach New York on Wednesday. Half of the convoy broke off and went to Norfolk. Clocks went back one hour.

April 27–Clear day. Chilly and calm. Approximately 80 miles out of Nantucket Light. Expect to reach the outside of the harbor tonight.

April 28 —Went into Brooklyn in the afternoon. Tied up to the dock. Received 90 letters and 6 packages. Had not received mail on this trip.

May 3–Off for home on a 4 day leave.

May 8–Returned from leave for a trip to Curacao and Ireland.

May 12–Left New York City about 1300. Picked up a convoy outside the nets. 12 tankers were with us. We are making about 17 knots.

May 13–Off the Carolinas in the afternoon.

May 14–Beautiful day–calm and hot. We're somewhere off the Florida coast.

May 15–Cloudy with a rough sea and rain. Off to Puerto Rico.

May 16–Very hot.

May 17–Clear and hot. Sighted land at 1500. P40 planes practiced diving on us. We laid off shore until 2200. Went into the harbor at Curacao off the north coast of South America. Climate is very hot with frequent rain storms and many coral formations.

May 18–Clear and hot. We tied up to the dock.

May 18, 1943

Dear Folks,

This is my first opportunity to write so I am writing you a few lines to let you know that I am well and feeling fine. I hope that everyone back home is feeling the same. I did not have a chance to write after I returned from my leave, but I arrived back to the ship safe and sound. I rode down on the bus to Philadelphia with a fella from Florence and he was stationed on the same ship that John worked on before he went into the Navy. If John comes home on leave in June tell him that I'm sorry that our leaves were not together so that we could see each other. I am going to try and write to him sometime this week. I'm wondering how Bernie is making out and where he's at now. I hope he likes it.

How are Pete and Butz doing? I'll bet they are glad that school is almost at an end. Tell them they had better study for their exams. How is Dad's garden doing? Are you getting anything from it yet?

I was on the sick list for two days last week with a bad cold and fever. I guess I had a little touch of the grippe. However, I'm feeling fine now. Ma, I opened that package you gave me to take back with me and Boy! those cookies and "sweets" sure hit the spot. I shared them with the fellows and have a little each night before going to bed.

Is Al still coming home? Tell him to send me a picture of himself when he writes to me. Also, tell him he should have joined up with a good outfit and see something of the world instead of stomping down sand dunes. I'll bet the kids are starting to go up to the lakes now.

Give my regards to everyone—Aunt Elise and Uncle Bill, also the Dietrichs &Hartmans. Tell Skin and Pete not to catch all the fish up at the lakes so I'll have some when I get home. Well folks I'll close for now sending you all my love and thinking of you.

May 19—Clear and hot. We slept topside at nights on the forecastle. Beautiful moonlit nights.

May 20—Clear and hot. We went ashore in Curacao. Bought some post cards and a Dutch newspaper. Got some Dutch money for souvenirs.

May 21—Clear and hot—stayed inside of the harbor.

May 22–Clear and hot. Underway at 0500 with a convoy of 15 tankers. We were at 14 knots going to Ireland.

May 23–Very hot and calm. Clocks set ahead ½ hour. It was steaming in both firerooms.

May 24–Clear and hot. Making 17 knots. 87 more days until I get off mess cooking.

May 25–Clear and hot with a smooth sea. Convoy fired. Clocks set ahead one hour. Approximately 12 more days to go.

May 26–Cloudy and cool. Approximately 1000 miles out. At 3:30 all work was stopped and the flag lowered to half mast. A burial at sea was held on the H.P. Jones for a fellow who was overcome by paint fumes in a basin locker.

May 27–Clear and warm with a smooth sea. 84 more days until I get off mess cooking. Clocks set back ½ hr.

May 28 —Clear and warm. We sighted a Spanish freighter on the horizon.

May 29–Clear and warm. The sea was like glass.

May 30–Clear and warm–clocks ahead ½ hr.

May 31–Cloudy and cool with rain. We are somewhere off the coast of Spain. USS Madison had sub contact this morning. We dropped two depth charges.

June 1–Cloudy and misty with a rough sea. About 350 miles off the French coast.

June 2–Clear, cool and calm. We're in an active sub area. The plane ahead of us dropped a depth charge on a sub. Later, a German blockade-runner fired on the plane. Destroyers Madison and Hughes went after the ship.

June 3–Cold with a higher wind and rough sea. Had sub contact in the afternoon.

June 4–In a gale with high winds and waves in cold weather. It cleared up in the evening. We saw some fishing boats the convoy singled out. Saw a life raft in the water. It was daylight until 2230.

June 5–Arrived off the northern coast of Ireland about 2300. Anchored at Moville and took on fuel.

June 6–We were underway in the morning for Londonderry. Arrived at 1000. Went on liberty at 1600 to the Red Cross building. Obtained some souvenirs and went to a dance at The Gill Hall.

June 6, 1943
Postcard
Londonderry

I'm well and in the best of health. How is everything at home?

June 6, 1943

Dear Folks,

Well I suppose you are all wondering where I am and how I am doing. I hope you received my letter a few weeks ago. I received your letter today dated May 17. I also received three other letters. One from Skin, Doris H. and Alice. That's one thing I am glad for, that we are receiving mail this trip.

I am well and in the best of health. I hope all you folks at home are the same. I just saw a movie on board tonight, it was called "Pittsburg". So now I am doing a little letter writing. How is everything at home? Is Dad still working late? How are the young chicks coming along? I'll bet Pete and Butz are glad now that school is almost at an end. Tell them both to study so that they pass.

Tell them if they do I'll treat them when I get home. Did John get home on his leave? I wish I could have been home. Skin said that George Banyas was supposed to come home. I guess he was glad to get home. I guess he and Skin went fishing together. I sure would like to have been there. Are Pete and Skin still as crazy as ever?

Ma, in your next letter will you send me Bernie's address? I guess you have heard from him by now. I would like to drop him a line. Ma, if you think of it, would you send me the Press once in a while and maybe Pete can send me a copy of the Review. Ma, when you write I think I will receive it quicker if you write by V mail. I'm now counting the days until I get off mess cooking. I have only three more weeks to go. I think I'll try and convince them to have an electrical dishwasher installed.

Well folks I haven't any more to write at the present so I'll close as I have to write a few more cards. Give my regards to everyone at home and remember me to them as I won't have time to write to everyone. I close sending all my love and thinking of you all.

P.S. Pete, don't forget to give the pigeons gris and peas. Give them a batch a couple of times a week.

June 7–Rainy and cold. Moored in the River Foyle at Londonderry. Daylight there until 2400.

June 8–Rainy. Went on liberty. Went to a dance at the Corinthian and Cryterian dance halls and learned the Irish jig.

June 9–Clear. Went out at 1300 for anti-sub exercises. We took the Marines to fire 20MM's.

June 9, 1943

Dear Folks,

I received your card today and was sure glad to hear from you. I'm really glad that we are getting our mail on this trip. You said that Bernie was at Sampson, NY but you didn't send his full address so in your next letter will you send it to me? Also, ask Mrs. Clauss for Ray's address and tell Pete to ask for J. Wilhelm's address. I bet the weather at home is pretty hot by now. I suppose Pete and Skin will be going swimming and fishing now that school is almost over. How is Dad's Victory Garden coming along? Did the old lady complain yet?

I sent out some cards yesterday, I hope that you will have received them by the time this letter reaches you. Tell Dad not to work so hard and to take it easy. I'll close for now thinking of you all and sending all my love.

June 10–Underway in the morning and went out again with the Marines. Fired 3" and 20MM's. Anchored at night.

June 11–Operated with a sub.

June 12–Underway in the morning for Curacao. We met the convoy at sea. Rough weather with high seas.

June 13–Cloudy with a high wind and waves. The ship was rolling and the waves were coming over the side.

June 14 —Clear and calm. We are somewhere off the coast of France near the sub bases at Loment, St. Nazaire. Clocks went back ½ hr. last night. 15 more days until I'm off mess cooking.

June 14, 1943
Postcard

Dear Folks,

Received your package. It was swell and I thank you alot. I'm on KP, that is why I'm only sending a card. Did you hear from Fran? I heard from Mrs. Hartman, but I can't answer with a letter this week. Thanks again. Write soon.

June 15–Clear and slightly rough.

June 16–Clear with ground swells. It's getting warmer.

June 18–Hot and slightly cloudy.

June 19–Hot and clear. Sighted a Spanish freighter.

June 20–Overcast. We fueled the ship.

June 21–Overcast and warm. We heard that we may go to San Juan, Puerto Rico instead of New York for repairs.

June 22–Clear and extremely hot with a calm sea. 7 more days of mess cooking

June 23–Clear, hot and calm.

June 24–Clear and hot. Sighted land in the the afternoon. PBY planes patrolling. I took the test for Fireman second class. I slept topside. It rained at night.

June 25–Clear and hot with a choppy sea. Made Fireman second class. Expect to arrive in San Juan Sunday morning. 5 more days until I'm done mess cooking.

June 26–Clear and choppy sea. Arrived at Aruba this morning. Going on a speed run to San Juan at 20 knots. We expect to arrive tomorrow.

June 27–Arrived at San Juan and tied up to the dock in the Navy Yard. Went on liberty.

June 28–San Juan. Mostly Spanish people. Had some fresh fruit and pineapples.

June 29–Frequent rains and hot.

June 30–Last day of mess cooking–Hurrah!

June 30, 1943

Dear Folks,

This is my first opportunity to write to you as we just arrived in port. I received your letters of June 3, 7 & 15. I also received two letters that Pete wrote. I didn't as yet receive the Press's you sent. I am fine and in the best of health. I just finished mess cooking yesterday. I believe it did me alot of good as I now have a heck of an appetite and weigh 160 pounds and beginning to fill out. All of my clothes are starting to fit tight.

I hope that everyone at home is all right. I'm glad that we are receiving mail when we reach port as it sure feels good to hear from the good old town. Tell Aunt Helen that I received her letter too. So far, I've only received one letter from Skin. I hope they haven't forgotten me.

I hope Pete and Butz made out all right on their exams. I guess they passed as they had good marks throughout the year. I'll bet they're living the life of Reilly now that school has ended. Well folks I'll close for today thinking of you all and sending all my love.

July 1–I went back to the fireroom and cleaned the boilers. We went to San Tuesci, another city in Puerto Rico.

July 1, 1943

Dear Folks,

Again I am writing a few lines to let you know I am feeling fine and in the best of health. I hope this letter finds everyone at home the same. I neglected in the last letter to tell you that I passed my exam and was advanced to Fireman Second Class with a $16 increase in pay. I'm going to put my course in for Fireman First Class next month.

I received a letter from Bernie dated May 30. He seems to like it alot. I hope he does all right for himself. He said he was going to try and get to school. I also received one from John saying he was being transferred to Charleston, S.C. How are Pete and Butz making out with their rabbits? Hey Pete how are your Bull Dogs doing in baseball this summer? Keep on writing Pete, I was sure glad to hear from you. Let me know the latest news and tell Butz if he gets time to try and write.

Tell Dad to take it easy working in the hot weather. Does he still have to work as late as 8:30? Well folks I'll close for now sending you all my love. Give my regards to everyone at home.

July 2–Hot and rainy.

July 3–Moved to the oil dock and fueled ships.

July 4–Went out to sea to fire 20 MM's.

July 5–Left San Juan for St. Thomas, Virgin Islands for gunnery practice.

July 6–St. Thomas VI. Operating with the new destroyers, 3 inch anti-aircraft guns and target firing. We fired at night with star shells and search lights.

July 7–Headed for Curacao.

July 8–Arrived in Curacao and fueled the ship.

July 9–Very hot. Went on liberty.

July 9, 1943

Dear Folks,

I have just come off the auxiliary watch in the fireroom and have finished my breakfast so I am sitting down to write a few lines. I am well, feeling fine and eating more every day. I wish I could be home to get some of those fresh vegetables from the victory garden. I'll bet its really hot at home now. I suppose Pete and Skin are living in the water up at the lakes.

How is everyone at home? Fine I hope. Does Dad still have to work late? I haven't received those Press's as yet. I guess I'll have to have my watch repaired again when I get home. I dropped it out of my dungarees and one of the hands fell off. I also had the misfortune of losing my wallet at the last place we were. I had only about $7 in it, but I didn't care about that as much as the picture I sent.

Well folks I hope I'll hear from you real soon. Give my regards to everyone at home and tell everyone I was asking about them. I'll close now thinking of you all and sending all my love.

July 10–Hot and rainy.

July 11–We got underway and picked up a convoy.

July 12–Warm and moderately rough.

July 13–Warm and calm.

July 14–Hot with a glassy sea. It was a beautiful moonlit night. We transferred over our doctor to a tanker to perform an appendectomy.

July 15–Hot and clear.

July 16–Hot and clear. We fueled the ship at sea. The Doctor returned to our ship.

July 17–Warm with a calm sea. This afternoon it started getting colder and rougher. Full moonlit night.

July 18–Cold and damp with fog. We're off the Grand Fishing Banks with our course now due east.

July 19–Cold. Clocks put ahead ½ hour. We had sub contact and dropped 6 depth charges. The Madison also dropped charges.

July 20–Foggy and damp with cold. Steaming in both firerooms 1 & 4 boilers. We were at 16 knots.

July 21–Foggy and cold. The clocks were set ahead one hour.

July 22–Cool and damp.

July 23–Foggy and damp. We arrived in Londonderry this morning. Received mail here.

July 24–Tied up to the dock.

USS Simpson
July 24, 1943

Dear Folks,

CENSORED and received your letters and all the Press's. I certainly was glad to to be able to get them. I enjoyed reading that column about the servicemen. I got "Fitz" Westphal's address from there. It was a sudden surprise to hear of Doctor Zwick's death and George Casey. I am in the best of health just now and feeling fine, but I have a little head cold. I was glad to hear that George Banyas got home. I wish I could have been home then. If you should ever see Al tell him to drop me a line.

Congratulations Pete & Butz for being promoted. I'll keep my promise and treat you both when I come home. How are the Bull Dogs coming along Pete? I see you are playing shortstop this year. How about dropping me a line once in a while. Hi! Butz, what are you doing during your vacation? Going to the movies I'll bet. How's your rabbits? The last I heard from John he was being transferred to Charleston, S.C. He didn't know whether he was going to stay there or get a ship. I have only one letter from Bernie and he was still in boot camp then. I hope Skin doesn't have to go. I wouldn't have anyone to go around with when I come home then.

Hello Dad. How are you doing these days? I hope you're not working too hard. I see by the paper that servicemen can get gas when they're home. ** Reverse page of censored sentence** Elise's letter and she said that you had a nice ham for the 4th thinking that I might be home. I'm sorry I couldn't be there, I could sure go for some of your good home cooking again. But I guess I'll just have to look forward to when I get home once more. Well folks, I'll have to close for now as "chow" is about to come down and that's one thing I never miss. I close thinking of you all and sending my love.

July 25–Clear and cool. Today I went to a little country church outside Londonderry.

July 25, 1943 (Postmark)
Postcard
San Juan, Puerto Rico

Hi Folks,

OK, feeling fine. Remember me to everyone.

July 26–Cool and clear. 6 old "cans" came in this afternoon. We are supposed to leave tomorrow.

July 26, 1943
USS Simpson

Dear Folks,

Here I am again with a few lines. Yesterday I had the opportunity to go to Mass. I was glad as I wasn't able to attend for some time. But every Sunday I always read the Mass from my book. Last night we had a movie on board. It was "Arabian Nights". It was good and comical in some parts.

Boy! Ma, I hope those young chickens are big enough to eat by the time I get home. I'm sure going to put on the feed bag. I miss that fried chicken. We've been having tomato salad the past few days and I got in an argument with a fellow. I bet him they were Jersey tomatoes and he said they were from Massachusetts. I'm always sticking up for Jersey. A fellow from Louisiana and myself have alot of fun arguing over which state is the best. I told him La. is nothing but swamps and he said Jersey had nothing but mosquitoes.

I wonder where Bernie is now, I'll bet he had some trouble at first getting up early in the morning. Remember when he was down last summer? According to his letter I received he likes it alot. How are the A's doing Pete? Are they holding down seventh place again this year? Maybe we can take in a game yet before the season end when I get home.

Well folks I guess that's all for now. I'll close thinking of you all and hope it won't be too long until I see you all soon.

July 27–Underway to fuel the dock. Cool weather.

July 28–Cool and overcast. We had anti-sub exercises and fired 20 MM's.

July 29–Cool. We had trouble with the main engines and rear gear. Found a small fire in the rear gear causing a loud vibration.

July 30–Underway at 1430 to meet the convoy. Overcast sky.

July 31–High winds, rough seas and high waves. Clocks went back one hour. I believe we are going to Curacao and then to the States.

August 1–Cloudy, rough and cold. It was steaming on #1 & #3 boiler and I had the 4-8 watch.

August 2–Cold and overcast with very rough seas. 600 miles off Newfoundland.

August 3–Cool, clear and calm. It's now getting warmer. Our course is due south.

August 4–Clear and warm. We're somewhere off the Jersey coast. Now making 19 knots.

August 5–Clear, warm and calm.

August 6–Clear and warm. We fueled the ship at sea.

August 7–Clear, warm and calm. The fireroom is now at 150 degrees.

August 8–Clear and hot with a calm sea.

August 9–Clear and hot . We are supposed to arrive in Curacao tomorrow.

August 10–Clear and hot. We arrived at Aruba, took some ships in and then proceeded to Curacao on a speed run of 25 knots.

August 10,1943
New York, New York

Dear Folks,

How is everyone and everything back home? I suppose all of you are roasting in the August heat. I'll bet Skin and Pete are living in the water at the lakes. How is everything at work Dad? I guess it's pretty hot there too. What have you been doing all summer Butz? Have you been giving "Spotty" a bath? How are your Bull Dogs making out Pete? Have they won any games lately?

I'm fine and in the best of health. I wish I were in the shade drinking a cold glass of Take-A-Boost right now. I still miss your good cooking Ma, especially my favorite chocolate cake. I read in your last letter about the surprise you had. I'll bet you sure were surprised, huh? I'll close for now folks thinking of you all and sending all my love.

August 11–Clear and hot. Left Curaco at 0900. Now by ourselves and making 20 knots. Ran into a convoy last night and was challenged by a destroyer. There were rain showers during the night.

August 12 —Overcast and cool.

August 13–We made a speed run on our way to New York. Increased the speed on 4 boilers until 31 knots was reached and then held there for 6 hours.

August 26–Underway from Brooklyn Navy Yard at 0800. Anchored off Fort Lafayette and took on ammunition. We put to sea at 1300.

August 27–Overcast and rainy with moderately rough seas. We are supposed to be going to Bermuda. We are traveling by ourselves at 20 knots.

August 27, 1943

Dear Folks,

Well I'm out on the big pond again and this is the first opportunity I have to write. I hope this letter finds everyone at home well and in good health. Did Skin leave Monday morning? I'm wondering how he made out. I'm not even home, but I miss him already. Send me his address as soon as you can.

Ma, tell Aunt Elise and Uncle Bill that I am sorry I did not call them, but tell them I was asking about them and I send my love. Well Pete and Butz, it will be a matter of weeks before you are back at school once more. Pete, did you get to go to Wildwood yet? When you go back to school tell the Chief I was asking about him.

How is everything back at work Dad? Is the weather awfully hot yet or have you finally had some rain? Folks, this is all I have time to write now so I will close thinking of all of you at home and sending all my love.

August 28–Arrived at Bermuda about 0900. Clear sky and warm. We anchored off the plane base. We had a swimming party for all hands in the afternoon.

August 29–Clear and warm. Held swimming parties in the morning and afternoon. Underway at 1430 with 3 other destroyers and the Carrier Santee. We're supposed to patrol the North Atlantic for subs.

August 30–Clear and warm. Carrier launched their planes all day. In the afternoon we practice fired at a plane.

August 31–Clear with a blue sky and warm. Carrier lost a plane in a landing this morning. Carrier fired in the afternoon. They sent torpedo and fighter planes up in the afternoon.

September 1–Clear, windy and choppy. The aircraft carrier lost a man overboard while the planes were landing. He was picked up by another destroyer. We fueled our ship from the carrier.

September 2–Clear and cool with ground swells.

September 3–Clear, hot and calm. Got a short haircut.

September 4–Overcast, calm and warm. Carrier lost another plane this morning. Picked up a convoy of about 86 ships.

September 5–Clear, warm and calm. Continuing with the convoy.

September 6–Clear and windy. We fueled the ship from a tanker in the convoy. Our position is now south of the Azores.

September 7–Clear and cool. We left the convoy which is going into Casablanca. We are continuing sub patrols into the Bay of Biscay.

September 8–Clear and moderately rough. We are somewhere off Spain. We heard the news of the surrender of Italy. Clear moonlit night.

September 9–Clear and rough. We are now in an active war zone.

September 10–Rough weather with high waves coming over the side. We are off the coast of France and in the tail end of a hurricane. We saw a twister last night. The sky is dark with thunder and lightning. A whale boat broke loose during the night's high winds.

September 11–Rough weather with high winds and waves. The carrier could not launch planes because of rough weather. The storm let up toward evening. We had a full moon last night.

September 12–Somewhat calmer with high waves somewhere off Portugal going into Casablanca.

September 13–Clear sky and warm. We saw a plane crash on a carrier deck. Beautiful full moon last night. We fueled the ship from a carrier in the afternoon.

Sept. 13, 1943

How is everyone in Riverside? I hope everybody at home is all right and feeling fine. I am fine, but just getting over a slight cold. We haven't received any mail as yet so I don't know of any news from home since I left. I am anxious to hear of Skin. Where did he go and how does he like Navy life so far? I can't write to him as I haven't received his address.

I suppose by now Pete & Butz are back at school again. I know how they just love to go back. Tell them to study hard this year so that they can again be promoted next year. Where did you spend Labor Day? Did some company drop in? I sure enjoyed the candy & cakes you sent back with me Ma. Every night I went on watch and took some with me and shared them with the other fellows. It sure was good. I hope I'll be able to get a few days at home next time so I'll be able to enjoy your good old cooking of three meals a day rather than just coming home at night.

One of the fellows had a birthday the other day and the officers cook made him a birthday cake and I had a piece. It sure reminded me of your cake making Ma. How is everything at home Dad? Do you have to work very late at night now? How is the old Chevy running? Is Butz still the No. 1 mechanic on it? Hi Pete, how is school? I'll bet it is pretty deserted this year. Are they going to have a team? Tell the "Chief" I was asking about him. I suppose you miss Skin alot, huh?

You should see me. I have a "whiffle" haircut like Pete & Skin. It sure feels cool around the ears. I'll try and write more later folks as I have to close for now. Give my regards to everyone at home as I won't be able to write to everyone. I close thinking of you all and send all my love.

September 14–Arrived in Casablanca, North Africa at 1045 and lay off shore until 1400. Jean Bart, a French battleship hit in the invasion of North Africa went out on a trial run today. We saw movies on deck last night.

September 15–Clear and warm. We anchored in the harbor. I had the 12-4 auxiliary watch.

September 16–Clear and warm, still in the harbor.

September 16, 1943
Postcard
Casablanca

How's everything going back home? I'm well and feeling fine. Remember me to everyone.

September 17–Clear and warm. We fueled the ship and took on stoves.

September 18–Clear and warm with a calm sea. We are underway again with a carrier.

September 19–Overcast and rough.

September 20–Overcast with white caps. We were patrolling around the Azores.

September 21–Overcast with rain showers.

September 22–Warmer. We met the convoy.

September 23–Clear and windy. We refueled from a navy tanker. I've been in the Navy one year today.

September 24–Clear with showers and calm seas.

September 25–Rain showers with ground swells. We have been underway one month.

September 26–Clear, calm and warm. We fueled the ship from a navy tanker in the morning and left the convoy afterward. Our course is now due east at 18 knots.

September 27–Clear and cool.

September 28–Clear and cool with rain showers.

September 29–Warm and clear.

September 30–Clear and warm. White caps on the sea.

October 1–Clear and warm. We fueled the ship in the morning and took on supplies from the carrier.

October 2–Overcast and cool with rough seas . The Allies captured Naples.

October 3 —Cold and calm. We slept with blankets last night. We are now in a concentrated submarine zone patrolling around the Azores within sight of land. Heard the news of a new acoustic torpedo used by the Germans.

October 4–Clear and windy. Heading southwest.

October 5–Overcast, calm and windy with rain showers in the afternoon. We met a convoy of 60 ships at 1330 and fueled the ship from many tankers.

October 6–Overcast and windy. We left the convoy and our clocks were set back one hour.

October 7–Calm and cool. We're now headed for the States.

October 8–Clear, warm and calm. We're now in the Gulf Stream. The clocks were set back one hour at 1900.

October 9–Clear, warm and calm. We're now 60 miles north of Bermuda.

October 10–Clear, calm and windy. The doctor operated on a fellow for appendicitis. There was a full moon. A carrier had radar contact last night.

October 11–Clear and windy with rough seas. Cerva was washed over the side at 0515 this morning. The ship took a 38 degree roll.

October 12–Clear and windy. A plane took off from the carrier with mail this morning and crashed into the water. We picked up a pilot, radioman & gunner and arrived in Norfolk, Virginia around 1500.

October 13–In the Norfolk Navy Yard.

October 14 to 19–Went home on 5 day leave.

October 23–Transferred from the USS Simpson on 23-day delayed orders.

November 13–Reported to Norfolk, VA for pre-commissioning training and 6 weeks in engineering school.

November 19, 1943
Norfolk, Va.

Dear Folks,

I received your letter yesterday and was very glad to hear from you. I have been pretty busy during the week. During the day I went out on work detail just to keep busy while waiting for school. One day I helped sweep out the gymnasium and ran a floor waxer. We were allowed to go up to the ships service store every night where we can get everything. Who do you think I saw there the other night? I ran into Joe Call from Moorestown. I hardly knew him he was so big. He was glad to see me since he knew I was down here, but he didn't know where.

I saw several good movies this week. "Lassie Come Home", "Northern Pursuit" and last night "The Iron Major" with Pat O'Brien. Well, this morning we finally got transferred out of the receiving barracks and now we're in Quonset huts while we are going to school. They are the corrugated huts. All the fellows from the Simpson are with me here. We're all together. All the fellows that are going on the Barton are together here. There are 225 of us. Now that we are all together we are getting more dope on what's what now. All the ship's officers are here too.

We are supposed to go to school for 4 weeks and then to our ship which is in Boston, not Maine, so I'm glad. I think it is supposed to go into commission next month. This week we went to classification where we were interviewed. They asked what we did on the last ship etc. When

I was finished they wrote on my paper a recommendation for a Petty Officers rating. I imagine because of my past experience on board ship because most of the other fellows here were never on a ship. We seem to have a good crew, I'm meeting lots of new fellows and making more friends. I imagine we will start school on Monday.

I received a letter from Skin. We are going to try and meet some weekend in Richmond. Skin cannot go outside 10 miles of Richmond. I understand we will have three out of four liberties and every weekend if we don't have watch. I heard that all of the firemen are going to machinist school. I was just going to put in for a leave this week while waiting for school. Now that we're all together and we start school on Monday I guess I'll have to wait until the ship goes into commission. Maybe we'll get some then. Give everyone my new address and tell them to write because I'll be settled for awhile now. I'll close thinking of you all and sending my love.

November 20, 1943
Norfolk, VA

Dear Folks,

Once more it's Sunday so we have the whole day to ourselves. I have just come in from washing some clothes and I'm dropping you a line before I go down to the ships service. Well, yesterday was our first day at the new huts. We had Captain's Inspection and therefore had to get all spruced up. Then we went to the drill armory and got our rifles. Yes, rifles. Everybody's singing "This is the Army now". We are supposed to use them when we march to and from classes. Our classes are supposed to start tomorrow.

This morning I went to the 10:15 Mass. I got up about 9:30 and didn't even eat breakfast. Sunday we can sleep as late as we want, but during the week we'll have to get up at 6 o'clock. We have a very nice chapel here. Sunday masses are at 0400, 0830, 0930, 1015 and 1100. We have mass every day at 6:20 and a mass at 4:15 in the afternoon. This Thursday on Thanksgiving I am going to communion as they hear confession every night and during Mass.

Ma, would you draw about $25 from my bank account and send me a money order sometime this week? They had pay day yesterday, but we fellows from the Simpson weren't paid as they didn't have our pay accounts straightened out so we'll have to wait until Dec. 5, the next pay day, to get paid. I had this weekend off (48 hrs.) and last night two of my buddies and I started out to spend it in Richmond. As our financial affairs were kinda weak we decided to hitch hike. We took a ferry to Newport News, Va. and then started out. We got two "hops" which took us about 30 miles outside Newport News and then that's all the farther we got. I'll bet 100 cars passed us and wouldn't pick us up. Now I know why the "Yanks" fought these "Rebels" in the Civil War. We had to hitch hike the other way back and a car took us to Newport News where we spent our liberty last night.

Next week if I get off I'm going to Richmond by bus and see Skin. We are going to meet at the U.S.O. One week he has Saturday off and the next week on Sunday. But he says I can visit him at the school any day after 1700. Well Pete and Butz, how's school coming along? How about the two of you dropping me a line sometime? Pete don't forget to let me know how Saturday's game with Bordentown came out. Don't forget to win the Turkey Day event. I'll bet you're going to have one of those big roosters, huh? I read in the "Seabag", the station's paper, that we're going to have a big feed and show on Thanksgiving Day. I sure would like to see that game with Palmyra, but I was lucky to get home last year as it was so you'll have to write and tell me about it. Well, as "Gabriel" once said: "I'd better blow now". I close thinking of you all and send my love.

November 22, 1943
Norfolk, Va.

Dear Folks,

Well, we had a pretty busy day. We were up bright and early at 0600. We had breakfast and then around 0800 marched to the drill field and had manual of arms and exercises with rifles. Then we went swimming. I guess you think I'm crazy huh? It was in an indoor pool. We were required to swim 50 yards then we had to swim to the middle of the pool, climb a rope cargo net, climb up to a platform, then lower ourselves and hang on the platform with our finger tips and let go and swim to the other end of the pool. Some workout huh? Even the fellows who couldn't swim a stroke had to go in. I made out OK.

After noon chow we marched to afternoon classes. We engineers went to the engineering school. A chief gave us a lecture about our new ship and modern boilers. Every Saturday we are to be given a test. Before we leave we will learn about boilers, superheaters, evaporators, turbines, engines, pumps etc. After class we had rifle exercises again from 0400 to 0430. The reason we are having so much training with rifles is because every Saturday we have a dress parade on the drill field before the captain and we are to do these exercises to band music. It really looks well with a couple thousand sailors all doing it in unison.

I have a tremendous appetite now doing all this during the day and I'm eating like a wolf. But I sure wish it was your home cooked chow Ma. We get fairly good meals here though. We also have WAVES on the base. They live in brick barracks down the street from us. Ma when you get those Christmas cards will you mail them as I'm kept pretty busy going to class 8 hrs. a day and I won't get a chance to send them. I think it would be a good idea if you put my present address on the back of the card so everyone can drop me a line and I won't have to send my new address.

BEAT PALMYRA

November 24, 1943
Norfolk, Va.

Dear Folks,

How's everything at home? Is it very cold there now? How's work coming along Dad? Don't work too hard. Is the Green Rocket still running? It's darn cold down here after sundown, but in the middle of the day its pretty warm. We wear gloves when we start out in the morning. Yesterday we were going to classes from 8 in the morning till 9 at night. Morning and afternoon we went to our engineering classes. At 4 o'clock we had rifle exercises.

After supper we went over to the pool again and practiced abandon ship drills. We had to climb the cargo net and jump off into the pool. I jumped in three times and made a regular swimming party out of it.

We attend engineering classes morning and afternoon and take down notes in class. We have a chief for a teacher and he's a comical guy. He's been in the Navy 25 years and has been at Pearl Harbor, the Battle of Midway and the raid on the Gilbert and Sullivan islands. I received Pete's letter and Ma's today. Boy Pete, I sure would like to have seen the 67-0 skunking you gave Bordentown. I sure hope you move on Palmyra the same way. So you had three quarters huh? Keep it up. Ma will you send me a few Press's when you have time? We're kept pretty busy going to school here, but we get a few hours at night to ourselves. Well folks the lights are about ready to go out so I'll have to sign off.

November 27, 1943
Norfolk, Va.

Dear Folks,

My section has unit duty tonight which means I have to stay in so I'll drop you a few lines and let you know how I'm getting along. We had to go to class on Turkey Day, but we had the better part of the afternoon off and all night. As you can see by the menu I sent home we had a pretty good feed. That night I went to the U.S. O. show at the recreation center and it was really swell.

Today (Saturday) we only had classes up to dinner. After chow we had to dress for inspection. We were inspected by a commander and then did our rifle exercises to band music and passed in review. We then turned our rifles in. You see we only had to march with them for our first week here.

We also had a test at class today and I received a pretty high mark. We are supposed to take a test each Saturday and the marks go in our record. When we go aboard ship the engineering officer will look at our marks and then pick the men he wants for certain duties. You can be sure I'm doing my best to get good marks. I think we fellows from the Simpson will do all right as we have the experience and have been to sea before. Most of the firemen and seamen are just out of boot camp.

I just heard that Navy beat Army today 13-0. Pretty good, huh? I just can't wait until you write Pete and tell me about Thursday's game. Ma, I received your swell package right after the big dinner on Thursday and also the money order. I shared it with my bunk mates and it really was swell. We have mail call after dinner and supper. I was glad to read the old Press too. I'll close for now thinking of you all and sending my love.

December 1, 1943
Wednesday

Dear Folks,

I received Mother's two letters, Paul's, Pete's and the Press's since Monday. I understand that you don't have much time Dad so Ma and Pete can give me the latest news. It has been cold here since Monday. Yesterday we had snow flurries that turned into rain. And this is supposed to be the sunny south. We still go to class from 8 in the morning to 4 o'clock in the afternoon. Last week we studied boilers, this week we're studying refrigerating machines, measuring instruments and pumps. We have a test each Saturday and personnel inspection.

We have 15 fellows to one of these Quonset huts which are heated with a big oil stove. They're warm too. We have a bunch of comical guys who always have us laughing. I was really surprised Pete when I got your letter that Riverside had lost. But that was a close score. I guess all the good teams lost last week. How about Notre Dame, huh? Ma, you could send your letters with a three-cent stamp as I get them the same time as Air Mail. It only takes one day from Riverside. You can give those pictures to anyone you want Ma as I have no one in particular in mind.

Boy Ma, that menu of yours was really something. I sure wish I was there to help eat it because the turkey we had was barely warm. I think we'll be up in Boston the week of the 18th. I'll be glad to get back up North. Boston is closer so I may have a chance to get home again. We have a darn good crew who are bunch of swell guys. The officers are a swell bunch too. So far, I think I'll have this weekend off. If I do, I'm going to try and run up to see Skin. The day before yesterday Secretary of the Navy Knox drove through the station. He came riding in a big car. I'll close for now sending my love to all.

December 2, 1943

Dear Folks,

How is everything at home? Is it very cold? This is really changing weather down here. One day real cold and today it was really hot. In December too. I heard from Bernie, he's still in California. He says he went into Hollywood on Thankgiving Day. We're still learning alot at school. In the last few days we studied refrigeration machines, condensers, pumps and evaporators. We have exercise from 4 to 4:30 in the afternoon. So far I think I'll have this weekend off. If so, I'm going to see Skin.

Last night I went to the early show and saw "Something About a Soldier". It was about officers candidate school. Then I went up to the gym and saw the opening basketball game between the N.T.S. and the seabees from Camp Perry. When I left the score was N.T.S.–60 and Seabees–40 in the third period. The captain and rear admiral of the base were at the game. Ma, when you get the cards will you send me one so I can see what they look like? I'll sign off now thinking of you all and sending my love.

December 7, 1943
Norfolk, VA

Dear Folks,

How is everyone at home? Is it very cold in Jersey? This weather is really changeable. One day we have snow flurries and the next day it's warm again. It was a beautiful day on Sunday.

Well I didn't get to Richmond again this week. I received a letter from Skin saying his liberty was changed and he wouldn't have liberty till Sunday. But this Saturday he'll have off. Friday I saw "Happy Land" at the canteen then I went to a "smoker" up at the gym. We were given sewing kits and cigarettes. We saw a quiz contest and boxing bouts. Sunday night I saw the Ritz Brothers in "Never a Dull Moment", it was really funny. Last night I went to see Henry Aldrich in "Henry Haunts a House". Butz, you should see this one, it's really funny. The N.T.S. basketball team skunked Camp Butner (Army) last night 75-20. We've had alot going on here lately. Last week Secretary Knox came through. On Friday an admiral was here on an inspection tour. As this is Pearl Harbor Week they had a big bond drive here. They have a "German jeep" that was captured in North Africa on display which they drive around the base. They also have German rifles, Italian rifles, camouflage hoods, mess kits and a propeller from a German Messerschmidt—all of which were captured in Sicily or Italy.

With every war bond purchase you get a chance on one of these war souvenirs. In front of the base movies last night they had station WNRA hooked up and the admiral of the 5th Naval district spoke. So you are a working man now Pete? Maybe you'll be manager of the 5 & 10 soon. Say Butz that was a swell letter you sent me last time. I sure was glad to receive it. Did you write it all by yourself? Write me another one sometime huh? Don't forget and write too Pete when you have some time. Well Dad how is work going? Is Christmas speeding it up any? Don't work too hard.

Ma did you ever receive any word from Washington about the insurance? When you send the Press's will you send the Reviews with it? Pete said he got another one last week. I'll sign off for now thinking of you all and sending my love.

December 13, 1943
Norfolk, Virginia

Dear Folks,

I received your letter and package. Thanks alot for the package Ma, those "goodies" were very good. Your letter was dated Thursday the 9th and I just received it so I guess the mail is starting to jam up already. It only used to take a day to get here. We have mail call 3 times a day and it's coming in bags full. Those Christmas cards are real nice, I like them a lot. We are supposed to leave here no later than Monday the 20th. You could send the cards down to me if you think I'll get them by then. Don't send any stamps as I can send them free.

All the dope we have so far is that the ship is to be commissioned sometime between the 21st to the 24th. So I don't know about getting home yet. We do know that we will be in about two weeks after its com-missioned loading stoves, parts assembly etc. Then we'll go out on the shakedown cruise which is supposed to take 4 or 5 weeks. If I could get a 48 hr. from Boston sometime I could get home. I'll give you a call when I get to Boston.

Well I guess I'm just out of luck getting to see Skin. One week I didn't make it hitch hiking, last week Skin had his liberty changed and this past Sunday we all went out into the Chesapeake Bay in an old can even older than my last one. It was the 144. It was just to show those fellows that had not been to sea, but we all had to go out. Last week we went to the fire fighting school. They trained us in the use of the different fire extinguishers on different type fires. Then we put on foul weather gear and actually put out fires. They set oil tanks on fire, a garage etc. and we put them out.

Tell Uncle Lawrence that I was asking about him and hope he gets well quickly so he can go out and get a deer on the 17th. It's really cold now. We stood inspection last Saturday with pea coats and gloves. I'll bet it's really cold up home now. Well Dad I suppose you will be busy working the next few weeks. I bet you look sporty in your new duds Pete. A regular dude, huh? Butz, I see that you were on the honor roll. That's swell, keep it up. I'll close for now sending my love and thinking of you all.

P.S. Did you receive any word yet about the service insurance?

P.P.S. I received the Press and Review the other day. Did you get that picture I sent last week of the two sailors? Put these pictures I am enclosing in the album. I'm enclosing a picture of two of my buddies who were on the Simpson with me. The one in white is Frank Cervo, the fellow we lost over the side last trip. The one in blues is from Chicago. He is here with me and going on the new ship. Put it in my album.

December 16, 1943
Norfolk, Va.

Dear Folks,

While I am writing this letter I'm almost freezing to death. Boy! is it cold. We had 4 or 5 inches of snow yesterday and it's still on the ground. The wind is howling and cuts your face like ice. To top it all off, we had to go out into the Bay again yesterday. I'll bet all of you are snowbound in Riverside if it's this cold here.

As I write this letter I am pretty darn discouraged. First we heard the ship was to be commissioned on the 17th for Boston. Then the commission was changed to the 24th. Now the latest dope came out yesterday that we will still be here on the 25th and the ship is to be put into commission on the 31st. So I'm between the devil and the deep blue sea. I don't know when I'll get home or if I'll get home at all. I don't think they know themselves when it's going into commission. So if I can get home you can expect me at any time because they've changed the date of the commissioning every few days. So I guess I'll have to just wait and see. How is everything at home? Pete still working at the 5 & 10? I guess Butz is all excited already with the Christmas season. I saw a few trees on sale here already. I'll close for now with love to all.

December 24–Arrived at the Frazier Barracks in Boston Navy Yard from Norfolk, VA.

December 24 to 27–Spent Christmas at home.

December 28, 1943
Boston, Mass.

Dear Folks,

Just a few lines to let you know that I arrived safely Monday morning. Although both trains from Philadelphia and New York were running late we made it on time. We took the 10:04 from Phila. and it was an hour late and arrived in New York at 12:30. We had to go into Grand Central and just made the 12:45 to Boston. We had to sit on our travel bags all the way to Providence, Rhode Island before we had a seat. We arrived at the barracks at 8 o'clock and they didn't call muster until 9 so we had plenty of time.

This is sure a swell place. We have nothing to do all day, but muster at 0900 and 1300. We can sleep till eight too. They have a swell canteen, it's called the Ingraham Club and named after the first sailor killed in the last war. The chow is excellent and we had a pie and ice cream dinner and supper. I think that Boston is a better city than New York. They have all kinds of U.S.O.'s and Y's here. We are going and try to get tickets for the Ice Capades this week.

I guess you'll receive the invitations to the commission the same time you get this letter. I know you can't possibly get here, but it's a good souvenir. Ma, when you get the packages will you put the Press in it? I close sending my love to all.

December 30–Put the destroyer USS Barton (722) into commission in the Boston Navy Yard at 1500.

December 31, 1943
New Years Eve
Boston, Mass.

Dear Folks,

Well I'm finally settled in my new home. The ship was commissioned yesterday afternoon at 1500. Everyone was assembled on the fantail and our Captain accepted the ship from the Yard commander. He's a swell fellow and an Irishman named Callahan. This is sure a swell ship, all clean and freshly painted. Alot different from the other ship and more roomier.

We know that we will be in for a fitting out period of two more weeks and then leave for our shakedown cruise. We hear that we may get this weekend off, but we won't know for sure. Boston is a swell city. The people here are sociable and treat all the fellows swell. It gets pretty cold sometimes though. The fellows that brought the ship down from Maine said it was 15 below zero up there. It was all covered with ice when it came in. Last night one of my buddies and I came out of the show and who did I run into but Johnny Getz. He was sure surprised and said it was the first time he ever ran into anyone away from home since he's been in the Navy. I received some late Christmas cards today, but as yet haven't received all the packages. When you send it, don't forget the Press's.

Well how is everyone at home? Is it still cold? We had snow flurries today. I guess Pete and Butz are sure enjoying their holiday vacation. I'll sign off for now and send all my love.

1944

January 2–Stood first watch (cold iron).

January 7, 1944
Boston, Mass

Dear Folks,

It's 12:30 AM and I've just come on watch. I have the 0000-0400 (12-4) watch and as we've been in dry dock there is no machinery running so I have a good chance of dashing off some letters.

The weather has been pretty cold lately. On Tuesday it snowed all day, but turned into rain and rained cats and dogs all day yesterday. Now it has changed again and it's snowing very hard. Have you had any snow in Riverside yet? I've received your packages yesterday (Wed. 6th) and wish to thank you loads Ma for the swell cookies, candy and the Press's. Only I haven't received any letters from you so far. All I had was a letter from Butz. I called up Tuesday night about 9 PM, but couldn't get any answer. I sure hope no one at home is sick or anything.

When I got the packages I took them down here in the fireroom and we put on some coffee to go with the cookies and fruit cake. The fellows really enjoyed it. We've been in dry dock the past few days and have no machinery running so all we have to do is keep the place cleaned up and learn about our new ship. Speaking of the ship, it really is a beauty. You don't mind working in a nice clean new ship like this.

I had a letter from Skin today. Boy is he lucky getting stationed at Philadelphia. I'll be he eats almost all his meals at home now. I'm putting in for a weekend pass today, but I don't know if it'll go through or not as an awful lot of fellows are putting in for it too. I haven't had much time to write since I've been here as we've been busy during the day and at night we have liberty or watch. Boston sure is a swell place, I like it better than New York. We get invitations to all kinds of partys, free tickets to shows etc. and the people are swell. I saw a very good picture the other night, "Thousands Cheer". Try and see it if you can.

Say Pete, can't you find the time to write to your brother? I had a very nice letter from Butz and he gave me lots of news. I saw in the Press about your football banquet. How's about writing and give me the low down on the basketball season and Reviews?

Are you playing ball at the Turners? I want to thank you for the swell letter Butz. It was real nice, see if you can get Pete on the ball and write. Well Ma and Dad have you taken the Christmas tree down yet? I suppose its pretty dry by now. Are you still rushed at work now that Christmas is over with Dad? I imagine we will be around Boston till the 16th or 18th. Then we will go on our shakedown run. I'll have to sign off now and write a letter to Skin. Have you heard from Bernie? Write soon–love to all.

P.S. Did you forget my box of stationary Ma or are you sending it separate? It wasn't with the other two packages.

P. P.S. Give my regards to everyone else as I won't have time to write to everyone.

January 12, 1944
Boston, Mass.

Dear Folks,
Well finally after 3 or 4 phone calls I got in touch with you. I sure was glad when I found out that no one was sick or anything. Its been awfully

cold here in Boston. It snowed twice since we have been here and each time it was about 4 or 5 inches. Some of it is still on the ground.

I put in for a weekend last week, but we were in dry dock and no one was allowed to leave until we were out of dry dock. We left it about five o'clock Sat. night so it was too late. If I could have gotten off at 12 or 1 I could have made it.

Our new ship is a beauty and everyone likes it alot. Even the yard workmen remark how swell it looks. Since we've been in commission, 2 Captains and 3 Admirals have come aboard from Washington to look it over. We are supposed to leave some time next week on our trial runs and will be away five or six weeks then come back in for a check up period. We may then have a chance to get some leave or at least get a couple of weekends. I can't say for sure where we'll go, but I have a darn good idea. I think the Carl boy from Moorestown went to the same place for his trial run.

I suppose Skin will have lots of chances to get home now that he's across the river. He couldn't ask for a better place to be stationed for awhile than Philadelphia. Boston is a swell town. All the people are sociable and swell to everyone. I can see the Bunker Hill Monument from the ship. Well folks I'll be closing for now thinking of you all and send all my love. Write soon.

January 14–We now have a two week fitting out period with dock trials, runs and full power at 35 knots.

January 15–En route from the Boston Navy Yard to the Washington, DC Navy Yard. With low water we had to secure the #1 bulkhead. The main fuel engine burned up and we had to proceed into Norfolk on one screw.

January 15–March 5–Laid in at the Norfolk Yard for repairs to the main engines. We made two trial runs in the Chesapeake Bay at 35 knots.

January 16, 1944
Boston, Mass.

Dear Folks,

How is everyone and everything at home? Is it very cold there now? Its just beginning to get a little warmer here, but it's still pretty cold. I had quite a jar this week. I had two booster shots for tetanus renewed which made my arm sore and stiff and thought that rigor mortis had set in. That was in the morning. In the afternoon I fell off the top of No. 1 boiler clear down to the floor plates, a drop of about 15 feet. I landed right on my bottom, hit my head on a tool box and bruised a muscle in my leg and shoulder. I sure was lucky not to have had anything broken.But I was sure stiff and sore the next day. Felt like I'd been struck with a truck. I went to sick bay and the "Doc" patched my bruises up. One of the fellows said that when he heard me hit the plates he thought it was a yard workman falling into the boiler. Ha, Ha!

We've been going out the last few days to try guns and had a full pow wow yesterday. And can she step. Everybody says it just looks like a baby cruiser. We went out today and it was a little choppy. About four or five of the new officers were throwing up. Ha! Ha! A seaman said to me: "Boy! look at that big wave coming" (it was a swell about two feet high). I asked him what he's going to do when it gets rough. Everytime we go out we always have a couple of commanders or other officers looking the ship over. Last week the aide to the aide to the President was aboard from Washington.

We are supposed to shove off some time this week for a trial run. I bet by the end of next week we'll be getting a good sun tan. I saw some good shows up here lately. "The Cross of Lorraine", "Whistling in

Brooklyn" with Red Skeleton. Last week Glen Gray and Vaughan Monroe were here. They were really good. I received all of your letters this week and was glad to hear from you again. Will you send the Press and Review Ma? I'll close sending my love to all.

January 26, 1944
Norfolk, VA

Dear Folks,

How is everything at home? Everyone is well I hope. I received Mother's letter yesterday and was glad to hear from you. I guess you are all suprised to see that this letter is postmarked Norfolk again. It was like this. We pulled out of Boston last Friday afternoon and originally headed for the capital. On the way down we burned up our main engines somewhere off the Jersey coast. I think it was around Cape May. Well instead of pulling into New York or Philadelphia we had to proceed on to this hole again. All the main engines are being lifted and I imagine we will be here two or three weeks. Boy if this were only Phila. or NY I could be coming home every night. Almost everyone is staying aboard ship in this dump.

This sure has turned out to be a good ship. Our laundry opened last week and now it's no more trouble washing clothes for me. We have our own library of about 500 books and a ship's service store. We're getting pretty good chow too. We can make our own ice cream on here. We also carry our own bakers and have plenty of pies, cakes and cookies. But Ma I still say that I wish I were back stealing your chocolate cake from underneath the cake pan.

On the way down I think that I never before saw so many fellows sea sick. And it wasn't even choppy. There were fellows staggering all around coughing over the side. Officers too. One fellow told me he was dying and couldn't walk. Ha! Ha!. There were only two mess cooks left on their feet and the chow line was practically a help yourself service. I don't know what those fellows are going to do when it gets really rough.

I met almost half the crew off the Simpson down here the other night. They pulled in last week too. It was good to see and talk to some of the old gang again. Well I have to write a few more lines so I'll be signing off for now. Love to everyone.

P.S. Say Pete did your fountain pen go dry again?

February 3, 1944
Norfolk, VA

Dear Folks,

Just a few lines to let you know that we are still in Norfolk. I imagine we will be here several weeks yet. The only thing good about this place is the climate. The past week has been just like spring. The temperature has been around 75 degrees and it's been the first time we could go ashore without wearing a peacoat for awhile. How is the weather back home?

We haven't been doing very much since we have been here. Every day we just do a little cleaning up in the fireroom and learn more about the operation of the machinery. This is sure a swell bunch of fellows. I imagine we will be able to go up for our next rate sometime after our trial run. Then I'll be able to wear my arrow. I received Pete's letter and Mother's this week. Also the one you enclosed from George and the Press's and Reviews.

How is everything back up in good ole Jersey? Are the chickens laying good now? What's new around town? How are you doing with your exams Butz? Have they been very hard? Vince are you playing any basketball? Riverside must be doing all right now with 6-2. Well Dad how is work just now? Are you being kept very busy? Take it easy Dad and don't be working so hard. Say Ma keep your eye on a big ole fat rooster in case I have a chance to get home while we're here. I really yearn for one of your super duper dinners again.

Well folks I'd better close for now. Hope I'll be hearing from you soon. I send my love and a big hug and kiss for everyone.

February 8, 1944
Norfolk, VA

Dear Folks,

I am dropping you a few lines to let you know that I arrived back in Norfolk safely. My bus to Philadelphia made it in 35 minutes and I had plenty of time to catch the train. I was in Norfolk at 9 o'clock Monday morning, had some breakfast and was back on the ship with time to spare.

I want to thank you again Ma for that swell dinner you had. It sure was a treat to be able to eat some of your good ole home cooking and desserts again. I opened the lunch you gave me when I came back to the ship and treated some of my buddies with those chicken sandwiches and chocolate cake. We all pitched in and had a big feed. Boy! they said "you must have a swell Mother to make up a box like this".

It's pretty chilly just now. Feels like snow in the air. The fellows said it rained all day Sunday. Last night we played basketball at the recreation center. The Engineers played the Communications Division (Radio Girls). We won 24-19. I played center and made a big four points. The fellow from Burlington played forward on the team. The "O" division beat the Deck Force 26-2.

Going down the River Road in the bus the other night one of the old busses passed and a sailor waved from the window. It was Dick Prager one of the fellows I went to school with. Everytime our busses have passed we waved to each other, but still didn't get to talk to each other. Well folks I guess that's all for now. I'll sign off with all my love to you all.

February 12, 1944
Norfolk, VA

Dear Folks,

How is everything back home? I'll bet you're snowed in now, huh? I heard last night they had five inches of snow in Jersey City. It has been cold and rainy all week. Today it is clear, but awfully cold out.

Well I'm back to my regular routine. Today we had Captain's inspection of below deck living spaces. I spend most of my off-duty nights at the Callahan Recreation Center playing basketball. We have a regular schedule on the ship. Monday night we are playing the Chiefs.

Ma will you send me my basketball shoes when you receive this letter? I'm wearing a pair of gym sneakers I borrowed, but slide all over the floor with them on. I think they are up in the cedar chest in our room. We have a new percolator in the fireroom. We all chipped in and bought it. Before we had to steam up the water, now we can make it in five minutes. I'll rate this coming week-end so I'm going to try to get off again. If Skin comes over, tell him to try and get the week-end off too. Well take care for now.

February 19, 1944
Norfolk, VA

Dear Folks,

I received your letters and the Press, but so far the package you sent hasn't arrived as yet. I'm sorry I couldn't get home this weekend because we had Captain's Lower Deck Inspection yesterday and today we are having personal inspection. I couldn't get off until Saturday noon and so it would be too short a time to make it home and back again. If we were only in Brooklyn or Boston I would have lots of time.

Well we are still in Norfolk. They just finished putting in our engines this week and so it won't be long till we leave this place. I imagine we will either go on our shakedown cruise from here or go back to Boston. I had a letter from Skin and now he's in Rhode Island. He said it's just like "boot camp" and he's sleeping in the hammocks. We still have our basketball schedule running. We have a couple more games to play yet. We won three in a row, but lost our fourth, 25-21. This week the Chiefs played the Officers. Boy! was that a rough game. While I was over at the Recreation Center the other night I met Mike Pfister from Riverside. He's going to Cooks and Bakers school here at the base. How's everything back home? Has the snow gone yet? I guess it was the first good look you had at snow this year, huh? I heard they almost had a blizzard in Boston. Have you heard from John or Bernie lately? I haven't had a letter from either one in a couple of months. How's the high school team doing Pete? Still winning? I suppose Butz got some good sledding in during the snow.

I want to congratulate you on your birthday Dad. I'm sorry I'm a little late and didn't get to send you a card, but I just can't remember people's birthdays. I knew it was this month, but didn't know the date. Well, I'll close for now. I send all my love to everyone.

P.S. (Sat. Afternoon)—I just received the package in this afternoon's mail. Thanks a million Ma. Your cookies were very good and the cake too. We finished off the nuts and candy real quick, but I saved the cake and cookies for in between for myself. I wouldn't send the basketball shoes now Ma as I have only two more games and they probably wouldn't arrive in time. If we are still here yet this weekend I will try and make it, although I don't know for sure as yet. Tell Butz I have his "crow" for him. If I can't get home I'll send it. So long for now.

February 21, 1944
Norfolk, VA

Dear Folks,

I'm now on the 8-12 watch in the fireroom, we are standing cold iron watches with no machinery running so I have a chance to do some letter writing. How is everything up in Jersey? Is it very cold? We have had on and off rain for the past week. Today it was pretty warm with the sun shining.

I had quite a surprise last night. I was down in the compartment writing and who walked in but two of my old buddies from the Simpson. They said they just came in and were in dry dock a few piers away. When they found out we were in here so long one them said "gosh don't you wear out your mooring lines being alongside the dock for so long". I told them yea we change them every six weeks, ha! ha! After we talked awhile I went with them to the ole Simpson and saw some of the old gang. I woke alot of them up and held reveille on them. Boy! were they surprised to see me. They said "are you off that 722 over across the yard"? Boy! that looks like a cruiser I sure wish I were on. There's lots of new fellows on there since I left. Alot of fellows have been transferred too.

I just saw a notice on the bulletin board which said that there will be no weekend leaves given out this weekend so I guess we'll be shoving off for a trial run. Maybe we'll wind up in Boston. Hey Pete! you're slipping again. Don't you have any news to write since I've been home? How about a line?

Being on shore for a long time must be doing me some good. I'm still gaining weight and now weigh 160 in my swimming trunks. I'll bet those last 10 lbs. were gained off that swell meal when I was home Ma. Boy! I'll never forget that. I'm even going to have to sell my tailor made blues because they're too small and fit me like a girdle. The pants are let out all the way and they still don't fit. Where are Bill and Ernie? I haven't heard from John or Bernie in quite some time. Well folks I'll be closing for now. I send my love to all and hope to hear from you soon.

February 27, 1944
Norfolk, VA

Dear Folks,

Its now two-thirty in the morning and I am on watch here in the fire-room. I have the 2400-0400 watch tonight (12-4) and so I have a chance to catch up on my letter writing. We have had some beautiful weather this past week. In fact it was almost hot on Thursday and Friday, but on Saturday it turned to rain. The latest "dope" is that we are supposed to be leaving on trial runs either Wednesday or Thursday. I imagine we will be be in the sunny South by sometime next week. Everyone will be glad to get out of this place again.

I saw the big carrier the Shangri-La launched on Thursday. She is only a couple of piers down from us. It was the first ship I ever saw go down the ramp. It was christened by General Doolittle's wife and took 45,000 pounds of grease to launch it. I received a letter from Bernie. He's in Coleta, CA and says he hopes to get a leave before he ships out again. I think his letter must have traveled half way around the U.S. because he mailed it to one of my former addresses. When you write again Ma will you enclose Emil and Bill's addresses? I lost both and I suppose they've been changed since then too. Also, see if you can get Ray's address from Mrs. Clauss.

How is everything in ole Riverside? Anything new? So the old "Lizzy" is in Banyas "dry dock" huh? I'll bet Butz is supervising the job. I guess he's already pestering Dad to get new "44" plates. How is school Pete? Have the new Reviews come out yet? How is work Dad? Are you still playing "jokes" on the fellows? Now take it easy and don't be working too hard. Ma will you send me a few more Press's when you get some together? Well I'll close for now folks. I have a few more letters to write. I send my love to all.

March 5–Underway for Bermuda for a shakedown cruise at 25 knots.

March 7—Rough sea and cloudy. Everyone is sea sick. Arrived in Bermuda and tied upto the repair ship Altair.

March 9–Went out on an anti-aircraft tracking at 35 knots.

March 11–Liberty declared in Bermuda.

March 12–Went out to sea and operated with an American sub.

March 12-15–Operated with a submarine.

March 12, 1944
Bermuda

Dear Folks,

I suppose you have been wondering why you haven't heard from me for such a long time. Well I've been pretty busy lately out on the "bounding main" again. We are receiving mail and when you write I think it will reach me quicker if you send it air mail. The last letter that I received from you was postmarked March 2.

I'm feeling fine and dandy and still have my big appetite. Ma I'm sure looking forward to one of your good ole special chicken dinners when I come home again. Well folks how is everything? Do you still have snow up that way yet? How is the "green beetle" running after it was fixed back at Banyas? Hi! Butz, how is school going, have you made the honor roll lately? Well Pete I guess it won't be long before you will be playing baseball now huh? Are the Bulldogs going to have a team this year? I haven't received the copy of the printed Reviews yet. Hello Dad how is everything going with you? Take it easy and don't be working too hard.

Have you head from John lately? Where is he now? Will you send his address when you write again? I haven't heard from Skin since I was in Norfolk. That place that Joe Call went to must have been a nice place. Say Pete if you see the Hartmans tell them to drop me a line. I wrote to them, but haven't heard from them since I was home last. Well I guess that's all for now folks. I'll close thinking of you and send all my love.

March 16–Torpedo runs. Fired on "fish".

March 17–Fired torpedoes.

March 18–Anchored in the government sound each day.

March 19–Fired torpedoes and five inch guns today.

March 20-30–Night firing with torpedo runs, anti-aircraft firing, damage control practice and speed runs. We operated at night with the

squadron leader in formation and practiced towing another destroyer.
Fired depth charges and had a personal inspection by the commodore.

March 27, 1944
Bermuda

Dear Folks,

At last I have some time to myself and a chance to do some letter writing. I would have written before this, but have been kept pretty busy lately. I received your letter of March 20, the Press's and the new printed Reviews. I had to laugh at the column where they called Pete "Sleepy Lagoon". We are receiving mail daily and so when you write I'll receive it soon. Will you send me more Press's if you have some saved Ma?

I'm well and feeling fine. At present I'm suffering from a case of sunburn. I hope you received my letters and birthday cards by now. Mother, I wish both you and Pete a very happy birthday and wish that I could be there to celebrate it with you. Well folks are you still snowed in? I suppose that was the biggest snow storm you had this year. Say Butz what were you trying to do play hookey and stay home with the grippe? I hope you're better now. How's your rabbit farm going Pete? Are the pigeons doing okay? How's everything at work Dad? Is the "green beetle" still running ok?

Can you still get camera film in Riverside? I've got two rolls for the big camera and one for Pete's. I had a letter from Skin and he said he was able to get home for a few weekends. He expects to commission his ship sometime in April. So George Banyas finally got home. I'll bet his mother was glad to see him. I suppose she was pretty sick.

What is John's address now? Is he still in Florida? See if you can get Ray Clauss's address for me from Mrs. Clauss will you Ma? Had a letter from Bernie and he said he was going to fly home on a 15 day furlough.

Well I'll have to close for now folks. Give my regards to everyone and tell them to write when they have time. I send my love to you all.

March 31-April 4–Fired five inch guns and had a damage control inspection. We expect to leave for Boston on Saturday.

April 4, 1944

Dear Folks,

Well I really hit the "Jack Pot" for letters this week. In the last three days I got 11 letters. I received all of your letters and cards Butz, Pete's and Ma. As yet I haven't received the packages you mentioned. I hope you received my letters and cards.

I'm fine and feeling dandy. My sunburn is just beginning to peel off now. I was ashore last Saturday and it was sure funny to see snapdragons, lilac and violets this time of year. Especially when you wrote and told me that you were just getting over snow. I spent my second birthday in a row on the water. We can celebrate all our birthdays together when I get home again. I'm looking forward to your good home cooking Ma. Some roast chicken and a chocolate fudge cake, mmmm!

How is everything at home now? Is Butz all over his giggles? So Pete's a regular working businessman now. Selling and working in a drug store. Dad, Butz told me all about getting the new license. I'll bet he even helped put it on the car.

I received a letter from George Banyas and he said he really enjoyed his furlough at home. Did Bernie get home for his? Skin wrote and said he expects to go to Baltimore soon. Well folks I'll have to close for now. Give my regards to everyone. Love to all.

April 6–Arrived in the Boston Navy Yard from Bermuda on Easter Sunday at 0700 with Navy and Marine passengers. Went on the second leave party.

April 20–Returned from a five-day leave at home. I'm now getting 3 out of 4 liberties. The Barton is in the dry dock. They're cleaning the boilers and punching tubes. It's also getting a new camouflage paint job. The weather is clear and cold.

April 20-22–Left dry dock and went to Pier 6. There was a ships party tonight.

April 20, 1944
Boston, Mass.

Dear Folks,

Just a few lines to let you know that I arrived here safely this morning. I arrived at 30th Street Station at 12:30. We pulled into South Station in Boston at 8:10. We had plenty of time to spare so we went to a cafeteria and had breakfast. Came on board ship about 10:30.

We are now in dry dock and have a new paint job. There is talk that we are supposed to hit another good port soon. I'll let you know later. Guess what Ma? Your long awaited package arrived. A little crushed, but everything in it was OK. My, I have so much stuff in my locker now it looks like a canteen. I'm on my way to go on liberty so I'll close for now until I have more to write. Give my regards to everyone.

April 24–It rained all day. We set the safety's on all boilers. Expect to leave at the end of the week.

April 24, 1944
Boston, Mass.
Monday night

Dear Folks,

I'm writing this letter here in the fireroom. I've just finished washing my blues, it's raining buckets full outside so I didn't go out tonight. It started raining this morning and hasn't stopped since. Both Saturday and Sunday were beautiful days, warm and sunny. Our ship has turned out well since the shakedown is over. All hands got five days leave, we are getting 3 out of 4 liberties and can get out at 2:30 in the afternoon to see the ball games. Saturday night they held a ships dance in the convention hall. Dancing, beer, sandwiches and even girls were furnished. Everyone including our skipper was there.

On Saturday afternoon we had off at one o'clock. They give free tickets to the ball games every day so I went to see the Braves play the Phils. The Phils won 3-2. On the way out to the park I saw Harvard U. and Boston U. I've seen quite a few historic places since I've been here. We are out of D.D. now and I think we'll be leaving here some time toward the end of this week. Have Hartman's heard anything from Skin yet? I haven't had a letter since I've been back from him, but I wrote one to him last night. I suppose he's left Baltimore by now.

How is everyone at home? I guess you're beginning to get some spring weather now huh? I'm sure enjoying those goodies Ma. I guess I told you in my other letter this week that I received your Easter package. It was a bit squashed, but everything inside was all right. I enjoyed reading those Press's even if they were a bit old. I was surprised to read about Godfrey Backus being a prisoner of war. No one even told me anything about it when I was home. Well I guess that's about all for now folks so I'll close thinking of you all and send my love.

P.S. When you write again Ma will you send me the following addresses: Ray Clauss, John's and see if you can get Allan Seiler's from Aunt Helen.

P.P.S. Boy! I had to get used to my bed here on the ship all over again. This one here is like a park bench compared to mine at home. So long for now.

April 27–Underway from the Boston Yard at 0800 going to Norfolk. Calm sea and warm.

April 30–Warm and calm. Had General Quarters and drills. Spotted a dead whale on the surface.

May 1–Arrived in Norfolk. Underway with another destroyer to Solomons, Maryland at 0800.

May 1, 1944
Norfolk, VA

Dear Folks,
    Well I still say this Navy really gets you around alot. Remember me talking to you from Boston on Friday night, well I'm back in Norfolk again. We left Boston Saturday morning and arrived in Norfolk on Sunday afternoon. So far I don't know how long we will be around or

where we are going after we leave. We were supposed to go to Brooklyn originally, but we wound up here.

The sea was calm as glass all the way from Boston. Today it was really hot. Already the uniform has changed to whites. On the way down we saw a dead whale floating belly up on the water. It looked like an over-turned lifeboat from a distance. I suppose that's why we went in close to investigate. I haven't had a chance to go ashore yet so I didn't see if I could see Skin's ship. In fact I don't really know if he's here yet, but I'm keeping an eye out for his ship. When you told me over the phone that he was here I thought that would really be swell if we met.

Ever since the Secretary of the Navy Knox died, all the ships in the fleet have been flying the flag half-mast since Friday. As yet, I haven't received your last letter or the Press, but I suppose I'll get them as soon as the next mail arrives. Your last letter was postmarked April 24. How is everything at home? Fine I hope. Have you had any spring weather yet? How's the garden coming along Dad? Does Butz help you take care of it? Thanks for your letter Butz, it was nicely written too. How's the drug business Pete? Say what vitamin pills are selling for this week? Ha, ha. Don't forget to give the pigeons a good fly and bath once in a while huh? I'm still nibbling on your cookies and candy yet Ma. The fellows are wondering where it's all coming from. Well folks I'll close for now, thinking of you all and send you all my love.

P.S. Ma don't forget John's and Alois Seiler's address. Did Bernie get transferred to Florida yet?

May 2 —Clear and calm. Anchored all night and practiced off shore bombardment. Left at 0100 and arrived in Norfolk at 0600.

May 3–Stayed in port. Trainees in destroyer training came aboard.

May 4–Underway at 0800 with trainees. Had drills and firing, returned Norfolk at 1600.

May 5-10–Took destroyer trainees out in the Chesapeake Bay.

May 7, 1944
Norfolk, VA

Dear Folks,

I guess you were surprised to learn that I was in Norfolk again. Well, we're still here. At present we are taking out "boots' for instructions until our squadron is formed. Friday I received your last letter and two Press's. Sure was glad to hear from you and read some home town news once again. So far I haven't heard a word from Skin since I talked on the phone with him over Easter. Did his folks hear from him lately or do they have any idea if he is still around here? I looked at every ship that I thought looked like his, but no #ARG 4. For once I was glad when I heard we were coming here for you told me his ship was in and I thought we would be able to meet each other. I finally heard from John this week. He says his new base isn't as nice as the last, but he likes it.

How is the weather up in Jersey? It has been awfully hot night and day since we arrived. Except for tonight because now it is getting a bit windy. We have been wearing whites ashore on liberty since May 1. It sure seems funny to be wearing them after wearing blues for so long. Means more washing too.

You'll never guess who I ran into on Main Street last night. I was walking down the street with one of my buddies and all of a sudden some sailor runs up and starts shaking my hand like a pump handle. It was Bill Reese. He was really glad to see me and says that I was the first

one from around here that he has run into. It's a small world. He's waiting for a DE in Orange, Texas.

How's everyone at home? Fine, I hope. I suppose everything is starting to turn green now. Already the foliage looks like the middle of summer. How is everything at work Dad? Do you have the garden pretty
well started? Well Pete and Butz it won't be long until school is over. I
wish you luck in your exams and hope you both pass. We had turkey for
dinner today, but Ma it never tasted as good as one of your super duper
roast chicken dinners. I sure wish I could sit down to one now. It's about
time for the lights to go out and so I'll have to say good night and send
my love. Give my regards to everyone.

*May 11–Went to Solomons, Md. Operated with a squadron in firing
practice.*

*May 12–Underway for Brooklyn at 0900. Took on ammunition,
stoves, and fuel. Went home on overnight liberty.*

*May 14— Mothers Day–Underway at 1000 with five other destroyers.
Met the convoy outside the nets. Fourteen ships carrying communications
and high octane gas. Clear, calm and cool. I hear we are going to England.*

*May 15–Clear and warm. We're heading due east. We practiced fir-
ing. Clocks moved one hour ahead. Now on 2400-0400 watch.*

*May 16–Clear and calm. We fired the guns today. Destroyer Julwett
joined us.*

May 17–Clear and calm. Clocks set ahead one hour We fueled the ship at sea. We are now southeast of the Azores.

May 18–Clear with white caps. The destroyer Merrideth joined the convoy today.

May 19–Clear and warm.

May 20–Clear and warm. Fueled the ship at sea.

May 21–Clear and chilly. Took exam for Fireman Third Class. Starting to get sub contacts.

May 22–Cloudy and cold. We had more sub contacts. The destroyer O'Brien dropped depth charges. I hear we are going to Plymouth, England. Some ships are going to Scotland. We are now 800 miles off Ireland.

May 23 —Cloudy and cold. I passed the test for Fireman Third Class. I was the only one out of five fellows to pass. Had more sub contacts. We're now 200 miles from the English Channel. We bursted steam on the #1 and #3 Boilers.

May 24–Cloudy and misty with cold rain. Arrived at Greenock, Scotland about 2200, one mile from Glasgow. Fueled the ship at 2330. Clocks put ahead one hour. We're now six hours ahead of States time.

May 24, 1944
Greenock, Scotland
V-Mail

Dear Folks,

A few lines to let you know that I'm well and safe and feeling as fit as ever. It's been some time since you've heard from me and as you probably guessed, I'm out on the Big Pond again. I'm sorry I didn't make it that Sunday, but I'm glad that I had the opportunity to get home for a few hours on Saturday night.

I just found out yesterday that I passed my fire exam for W.T. 3/c. I'm a third class petty officer. How is everyone at home? All in good health I hope. I suppose it won't be long before Pete and Butz are through with school and home on summer vacation.

Have you heard from Skin lately? Is he still in Virginia? I haven't had a letter from him since he's been out on the ship. If you should run into Hank Mitsch or Lawrence Yearly tell them I was sorry I didn't see them when I was home. Ma, will you send me some Press's when you have the chance? I'll have to close for now thinking of you all and sending my love. Give my regards to everyone and tell them to write often.

May 25–Clear and cold. Left the Clyde River at 0320 with the other destroyers. We picked up a convoy of twelve transports full of soldiers and eighteen destroyers going to Plymouth, England.

May 26 —Cloudy and misty. We dropped depth charges today.

May 27–Thick flag was posted because of a possible submarine attack. Went to General Quarters and dropped depth charges. We're now

85 miles from France. We arrived in Portland at 0400. We left the convoy and took one transport to Plymouth.

May 28–Thick flag posted . We arrived in Plymouth and anchored in the harbor. Condition "Red" during the night.

May 29–Clear and warm. There are lots of barrage balloons over the city. We had another air raid during the night. The bombers passed over the city on their way inland.

May 30 —Clear and warm. It gets dark at 1830. We went out with a squadron on maneuvers. We were made squadron leader of Devon 60. We now have a Commodore Freezeman and Lt. Commander Robert Montgomery aboard.

May 30, 1944
Plymouth, England

Dear Folks,

How is everything and everyone at home? I hope this letter finds all of you in good health. I'm fine and feeling well. We haven't received any mail as yet, but write often and then I'll have alot when it catches up with me. Don't forget Pete and Butz. Did you receive my other letter of May 24th? I'll write whenever I have the chance so don't worry.

I'll bet it's getting nice back home now huh? How is the garden getting along Dad? Well Pete and Butz it won't be long until you have a vacation. I wish you both luck in your exams. Are you still the town's number one druggist Pete? I haven't received that package you sent Ma, but maybe it will catch up with me. I wouldn't send any more as it will take me too long to receive then. However, I would enjoy some Press's and the Reviews if you can send them.

Have you heard from Skin and John lately? Has Skin had his address changed or is it still the same? You probably noticed I haven't said much, but I can't due to censorship regulations. I'll close for now thinking of you all and send all my love. Give my regards to everyone at home and tell them to write.

May 31 —We stayed anchored in the harbor all day.

June 1–We went out to sea with a squadron to practice shore bombarding.

June 2–Clear and cool. We fueled the ship from a tanker. Many landing crafts full of soldiers are now in the harbor. We took off all the paint and personal records in the afternoon. We believe the invasion is to start soon.

June 3–Clear and warm. We were underway at 1330 from Plymouth, England. We started forming an enormous convoy of LCT's, LCI's, and LST's (landing crafts) all night long. The coastal guns fired a salute as we left the harbor.

June 4–Clear and cold. The English Channel is very rough. We're still picking up invasion craft. The convoy now stretches from horizon to horizon in three columns. We are now patrolling along side to keep them in formation. The invasion craft are loaded down with tanks, trucks, jeeps, derricks and equipment. In the afternoon, one LCT started to capsize. We went along side and took aboard 34 army personnel. In the evening, word was received that the invasion was delayed 24 hrs. due to rough weather in the Channel so we put into Weymouth, England with the convoy at 2300.

June 5–Underway from Weymouth at daybreak with the convoy. Cloudy and cool. In the afternoon, we are now twenty miles from the French Coast. A floating mine was sighted and sunk at 1700. The Channel is full of floating mines. A minesweeper in the convoy hit a mine and sank at 2100. Thousands of planes are now going over and bombing the coast. Huge fires were sighted ashore at 2400.

June 6–"D" Day–"H" hour was at 0630. We are now about one mile from the French Coast and moving in with the other destroyers under the fire of the battleships Arkansas, Texas & Nevada. The battleships are now concentrating on the concrete pill boxes with 14" guns. We are now moving in closer to the beach and drawing fire from the pill boxes. We went to General Quarters at 0500 and remained there until 1900 firing steady at the shore installations. In the afternoon, our whale boat was sent in to pick up army casualties on the beach. When they landed they were strafed by German machine guns and had to come back out. The boat returned full of holes and Bacon Plum was hit. A soldier in our boat was hit on the helmet and knocked unconscious All during the night battleships and cruisers fired at the beach.

June 7–Clear and cool. Daylight disclosed all kinds of ships here in the harbor–battleships, cruisers, destroyers, patrol craft, PT boats, LCI's, LCT's & LST's and Higgins boats. We are now about 800 yards from the beach and can see the village and cliffs & rolling green hills. The Germans are concentrating artillery fire all along the beach. The Higgins boats & LCM's are trying to make a landing. Some were hit and exploded. Shells are dropping all around them. Some tanks are now moving along the beach. Several LCI's & LCT's are burning along the shore. Battleships & cruisers are still firing at the pill boxes and artillery concentrations beyond the ridge. When we moved in to shell the town we were fired upon by coastal guns. We were credited with two direct hits on concrete pill boxes.

June 8–Clear and cold. Went to G.Q. at 2435 last night for an air raid. A German fighter dove on our ship and began strafing. We opened up with eighteen rounds of 5 inch and were credited with shooting down the plane. At 0200 we lay down a heavy smokescreen for the battleships & cruisers. I awoke at 0600 and the compartment was thick with smoke from the smokescreen generator. Several bombs were dropped near the ship before daybreak. All the houses along the beach now show the telling effects of the bombardment. As I was coming off watch at 0330 I saw heavy anti-aircraft fire and saw a plane shot down over the beach. In the morning we were called to concentrate fire on German machine gun positions on the other side of the hill. All kinds of debris are now floating in the water–boxes, soldiers bodies, equipment and invasion craft, etc. During the night the destroyer Merrideth was hit by a torpedo from a German submarine boat. While being towed back to England by tugs, she capsized and sunk. The Nelson & Conroy were previously hit by shells from shore batteries. Lots of Mustangs, P-38's & Spitfires now over the coast and strafing machine gun nests in the woods. We have landed near the village of Caen on the Cherbourg peninsula.

June 9–The 34 soldiers we picked up in the Channel and had aboard were put off on an English ship at 0800. The French flag is flying from the flagstaff in the village. There were also two French cruisers anchored near us. We can still hear artillery & mortar fire from the shore. At 1930 we went to the outer screen to patrol. E-boats were reported there last night. Went to G.Q. at 2030 for air attack, but didn't fire. At 2345 another air attack with alot of AA fire. Six enemy planes were shot down by ships in the harbor.

June 10 —Clear and cold. Last night a lookout reported a torpedo just missing our bow. We fired at the concentrations again in the afternoon.

June 11–Clear and cold. Had G.Q. for two air raids again last night. Heard bombs fall and shrapnel hit the ship.

June 12–Had E-boat attacks again last night. We patrolled in the outer ship screen. Warm and sunny day. Several small fishing boats containing French men, women and children came out to the ship begging for food & clothing. The fellows gave them bread, candy, cookies, peanuts & cigarettes. With cries of Merci! Merci! they threw flowers up to us. They looked very hungry and starved. Last night a German destroyer was reported trying to pierce our outer screen.

June 13–Clear and chilly. There was another air raid over the beach last night. An LST was hit by a bomb. We laid at anchor most of the day to conserve fuel.

June 14 —Clear and cold. There were air raids again last night and in the morning. We counted fourteen searchlights in the sky, amidst flames and AA fire and bursting bombs. The Germans are now reported to be using radio controlled bombs & mines.Small minesweepers swept the anchorage before we got underway.

June 14, 1944

You haven't heard from me in quite some time now, but we've been busy with the war lately. I suppose you read in the papers where we gave them some h___. I'm well, feeling fine and hope all of you at home are the same. This is my first opportunity at writing. I don't know how soon you will receive this, but I hope it will be soon. I haven't any time to write anyone else so give them my regards and tell them to write. We haven't received mail as yet, but keep writing as I'll have plenty to read when I get to it. Due to censorship I can't say much now, so I'll close sending my love to you all.

June 15–Another air raid last night. Big display of AA fire. We had patrol duty again. Our fuel supply is getting low.

June 16–Another big air raid on the beach during the night. A big convoy of Liberty ships came in during the night. We went along side the Texas and fueled at 1900.

June 17–Clear and cool. Weighed anchor in the morning and proceeded to a point farther up the coast near an island lighthouse. Saw the Arkansas, Texas, Nevada, Tuscaloosa, Quincy and Augusta. We anchored until 2000, then went out to patrol in the outer screen through the convoy.

June 18–Clear and warm. We're at anchor next to the Augusta and off the beach head. I looked at the beach through glasses and saw encampments of tents, tanks, trucks and airfields. I heard today that Tokyo was bombed again for the second time since Doolittle's raid.

June 19–Cloudy and cool. We stayed at anchor off the beach most of the day. At 2400, when we were on the patrol in the outer screen, German planes attacked the ships in the harbor and dropped torpedoes. They were fired on by the ships.

June 20–Cloudy and misty with rain. Rough weather and visibility poor. We patrolled during the day and at night.

June 21–Cloudy, cool and rainy. Anchored offshore during the day. News broadcast said that Yank troops are three and a half miles from the city of Cherbourg. Heard that some of the resistance on the beaches was from women snipers. A message was received from the invasion commander and said that shelling of the beach from the fire support group was very effective. Many pill boxes were knocked out.

June 22 —Cloudy and cold. Anchored off the beach during the day. Underway at 2300 with the Quincy, Tuscaloosa and two English cruisers. Arrived at Portland, England at 0700. We tied up along side the Tuscaloosa. I met George Nowicki of Riverside on board and we spent the day together.

June 23–Clear and warm. We burned all day in the fireroom. Held reveille at 0300, got underway, but returned to port again.

June 24–Clear and warm. The Allies are now two miles from the city of Cherbourg. I hear we are going to shell it soon. Underway at 2230 and went outside the sea wall and anchored. Pulled anchor at 0300 and got underway with the Texas, Arkansas and nine other destroyers.

June 26–Clear, very warm and calm. We arrived off the French coast at 1100 and started shelling the city of Cherbourg at 1230. I was sitting by the depth charge rack on the fan tail when the German shore batteries fired on us. We were the lead destroyer in the battle formation and were straddled with a 4 shell salvo, one landing about 20 feet away and soaking me with salt spray. One hit near the bow, one went over and one 8" shell entered the diesel generator room. It hit about six inches above the water line, but failed to explode. The hole made by the projectile was big enough to walk through. This was just about four feet from my bunk. The repair party threw the projectile out the same hole it came in. Then they had to shore it up with mattresses, blankets, pillows etc. Fuel oil was all over the compartment about five inches deep. After the shore batteries opened fire, all the ships cut loose and fired at once while the shore batteries continued to straddle us with salvos. The destroyer then lay down a heavy smoke screen to protect the battleships. After bombarding the shore for three hours we returned to Portland, England for repairs and tied up to the repair ship Melville. The Texas, Laffey and O'Brien were also hit. An eight inch shell exploded on the O'Brien's bridge killing fourteen men.

June 26, 1944

Dear Folks,

I hope you will soon receive my letters. We received our mail for the first time in six weeks. I received all your letters from May 11th to June 15, but you said you still have not heard from me. My first letter was dated May 24. Most of the other fellows said their folks have not heard from them yet either after having written a month ago. So I suppose it's just due to the mail moving slowly.

I'm fine and in good health. Today I met a fellow from Riverside. He was George Nowicki whom I used to attend school with and we met accidentally and neither of us had any idea that we were so close to each other. He married Charlotte Johns of Riverside and has a little boy.

We both went to confession, heard mass and received communion together. The rest of the day we spent talking about Riverside and old times. He also said everyone laughs when he receives the Press as it's so small compared to the larger city newspapers. How is everything and everyone at home? Fine and well I hope. Have you heard anything from Earl McChynent? I'll bet you're having some swell days at home right now. I hope all of you will have a good time on your vacation Dad. Take it easy, relax and don't worry too hard. How is the garden coming along?

Congrats Pete and Butz on passing the exams. Boy! before you know it you'll be in high school Butz and Pete will be graduating. How do you like your job Pete? How are you doing during your vacation Butz? Going to movies and watching Banyas work on cars I suppose. Are you going to take Spotty down to High Point to swim? How are you doing Mother? I hope you haven't had any more grippe.

Take it easy and enjoy the summer days when it's hot. You sure made my mouth water when you described that dinner you had prepared for me when you expected me last month. Chocolate cake and all mmmm! But Ma, I hope it won't be long when you will again make one of your super duper dinners for me. Well folks I'll have to close for now. In closing I'm thinking of you all and send all my love.

June 26, 1944

Dear Folks,

Just to let you know I'm well and OK so don't worry. I have to thank you Ma for all your prayers and vigil lights for they sure helped us lately as we had some close calls. I hope everyone at home is feeling all right. I would like to be sharing some of that Jersey sunshine with you. How is the old swimming hole Pete? I'll bet it's nice on those summer days. Well in a few days you'll start your vacation Dad. Where are you going, North Jersey or High Point? I hope you all have a good time. I wish I were spending it with you.

Sure was surprised to hear John P. was home again. Heard from Skin in a letter dated May 31. First time I heard from him since Easter. Also had a letter from Bernie saying he and John met in Florida. Give my regards to everyone in the family for me as I will not have time to write to them. Save the Bulletins and Couriers at home will you Ma? In closing I send my love to all of you.

June 28-29–Along side the repair ship getting repairs to the shell hole.

June 28, 1944
Western Union Telegram
To: Mrs. John Yearly
Riverside, NJ

I'm well and all right. Don't worry. Love to all.

June 29–Clear and cold. Underway from Portland, England with the Tuscaloosa, Quincy and Texas.

June 30–Arrived in Belfast, Ireland. We fueled the ship then went ashore in Belfast on a 48-hour pass. I saw the town and interesting sights while on liberty.

July 2–Clear and cold. Underway with the squadron. We're going back to the states for repairs.

July 9–Clear and very hot. We arrived at the Boston Navy Yard.

July 10-23–I went home on a 13–day leave.

July 9–Sept. 16–In for repairs, cleaning boilers, painting the fire-rooms, straightening booth shafts and a new paint job. We went out into the Bay for two speed runs at 35 and 36 knots.

Boston, Mass.
July 24, 1944

Dear Folks,
 A few lines to let you know that I arrived safely and in plenty of time. I caught the 1:18 from 30th Street and arrived in Boston at 8:20. I had a good car and slept most of the way. First I had some breakfast and went back to the ship around 9. Was I surprised to learn that liberty started at

9:30 and my section rated liberty. So I was on the ship about 15 minutes, put my bag in the locker and went into Boston.

Hank, a couple of other fellows and myself went to Revere Beach and spent the day. We went in to swim and the sun was hot and the air warm, but the water was ice cold. It was the first chance I had to swim in salt water since March in Bermuda. I'll bet there must have been a couple thousand people out there yesterday. All day people were jammed on the trolleys. It's just like the shore with all kinds of amusements, roller coasters, etc. Boy! we had a swell time. Around 8 o'clock we came back to town and went to see a movie. We saw "What a Life" with Donald O'Connor. We saw the Frankie Carlyle Orchestra and on stage was Homer Brown–Henry Aldrich's sidekick in person. He was really funny. Butz would have enjoyed him.

Well I'm just getting back into the Navy routine again now. Sure was tough rolling out at 6:30 this morning. They're feeding us pretty well while we're here, but it doesn't even compare like your meals at home Ma. I really miss them now. I had about 20 letters waiting for me when I came back, but I didn't receive any Press's or packages. Ma, by the time you receive this letter my financial standing will be pretty low so will you draw $20 from my account and send it to me? Our paymaster is on leave and we don't know how soon we'll be paid. Well I'll close for now folks as I've got to get caught up on my letter writing. All my love.

July 31, 1944
Boston, Mass.

Dear Folks,

Arrived here on ship about 8:05 this morning. We took the 1:06 from Trenton and came into South Station 5 minutes to eight. Then we took a cab back to the ship. I received four Press's and your last letter this morning. They're gradually catching up to me I suppose.

I'm now writing this letter on watch in the fireroom. The 12-4 watch always seems so long so I take up time and catch up on my letter writing. We came into dry dock this afternoon. I imagine we will be here at least three weeks yet. We are about through with most of our repair work in the fireroom. Right now we're repacking valves, cleaning up, etc. I'm sorry I missed you Sunday night Pete, but at least I got to talk to you over the phone anyway. Did you enjoy your stay in Egg Harbor? I'll bet you're alot darker from the salt air too. Hank and I went swimming up to the lakes on Sunday afternoon. The water was swell. We left our trunks on the ship so we had to rent some.

Well Ma, you have another boarder this week huh? You should have lots of help now with Donald and Butz. Today was another hot day. They must have sold at least 80 cases of Coke. In the morning a truck came to ship, unloaded a truck full of Coke and took away a bunch of empty cans. Pete I guess I forgot to tell you–they have dog races up here too. They're held out at Revere Beach. Maybe I'll have a chance to see them before we leave.

Thanks again for the swell dinner Ma. That's the trouble with going home, you always have to leave again. But I hope it won't be long before I'll be able to stay at home once more and eat your swell cooking. Don't work too hard in this heat Dad, take it easy. I hope you'll get a good rain for your garden soon. I'll sign off for now folks as I have some letters to get out. Love to everybody.

P.S. Mother enclosed is $20. When you write again let me know if you receive it.

August 4, 1944
Boston, Mass.

Dear Folks,

I received a letter and the package of Readers Digests this week from you and a couple more Press's. Did you receive my letter earlier this week? We're now in dry dock and they're giving us a new paint job and scraping the bottom. They've cut out the plate where the shell entered and now have half the side of the ship's plates out so they can put the new one back in place.

Since I've returned we haven't had too much work to do in the fire-room, just cleaning up and everything. Boy! we sure had alot of fun the last few days down here. Chasing one another with air hoses, throwing buckets of water on each other. We really have quite a gang, comedians and all.

It's been quite hot the past few days with occasional rain showers now and then. I'm going to switch to whites tomorrow. Last night a few of the fellows and I went out to the Esplanade in Boston. It's a swell park along the Charles River. There is a big open air band stand there and they have band concerts every night. It was swell with a cool breeze blowing, sitting on the grass listening to the music. Night before last we saw "Four Jills in a Jeep". Last night I ran into a fellow up town that I went through "boot camp" with two years ago. He's on a ship in the Navy Yard. Also, this morning one of the fellows told me a fellow from my home town was aboard looking for me. He said he was going to radio school in Boston. I don't have any idea who it was, but maybe I'll see him yet.

How is everything at home folks? All right I hope. I sure do miss it after being home so long. How is you star boarder and Butz getting along this week Ma? Are you still going swimming Pete? How is work now that you're back again? I suppose football practice will start soon. Are you still taking care of the chickens all right Butz? How is your garden holding up Dad? Ma, will you send me this week's Press? Did you get those prints back from Fraunce's yet? Well I'll have to close for now folks. Hope to hear from you real soon. All my love to you all.

Postcard
August 15, 1944
Boston, Mass.

Dear Folks,

Hank, a couple of fellows, and myself spent Sunday here. We had a swell time. Water was fine. I'll bet there must have been a couple thousand people on the beach.

August 15, 1944
Boston, Mass.

Dear Folks,

Received your letter yesterday dated Aug. 11, also had one from Butz a few days ago. Sure was glad to hear from you. I just missed getting home this past weekend. I put in to get off at 11:30 Saturday, but the chief engineer caught some fellows in the engine room sleeping during working hours and so none of the engineers could get off until 6 o'clock at night.

By the time I got home it would have been time to go back again. How is the weather? Baking hot I suppose. It has been awful here the last 3 or 4 days. On Sunday it was 101. Hank and I went to Revere Beach for the day. Boy! that water was really swell. There were so many people it took us an hour to rent a locker and a suit. They're just about finishing work on the ship and we're supposed to get out of dry dock tonight. I think by the end of the week we'll be making trial runs. Today we have been in the yard just 35 days. Boy! the time has really flown by since then. Did I tell you in my last letter that I saw Bill Reese here last week? His ship was down two piers from us and he came aboard a couple of times.

How is everything at home? I really had to laugh when I received your letter telling me about Butz and Donny. They really must be a pair. Have you started football practice Pete? And are you still working in Paramount? Drop me a line when you have some time. Is the garden still holding out Dad? I guess everything's about done now. How did you like your swim at the shore Ma? You must really be daring if you went above your ankles. If you see Uncle Lawrence thank him for me for his package. It just came through this week, but was pretty intact. I'll bet it must have gone around the world since he sent it. I'll close for now folks. All my love to you all.

August 20, 1944

Dear Folks,

How is everyone and everything at home? Fine I hope. I received a letter from Dad and Ma and a Press (Aug. 3) on Saturday. Say Dad the day I received your letter we had a thunderstorm and it rained all that night. But thanks for the letter anyway. My the weather up here has certainly changed alot since last week. All last week it was scorching hot and one day the temperature was 104 degrees. We had thunderstorms Friday and now it is beginning to get real cool. It must seem like heaven around the house to you this week with Butz on vacation. Especially after having he and Don together. I wonder how he's doing since it's his first time away from home.

Our yard time was supposed to be on the 17th of last week and we went out on sea trials Friday. They found a few things wrong and we are in dry dock again and expect to have 8 or 10 days. Our shaft was so many thousands off and they have to take it out. Today is our 40th day here. Boy! it doesn't seem that long at all. That's the longest I've been on the beach since I can remember. I missed coming home this weekend as I had the duty. I think Hank was going to try and make it as he rated the weekend. We're in different sections now, he's in 1st and I'm in 3rd. They changed the berthing arrangements on the ship and now he sleeps right under me.

Did you see in last week's paper the article on the "Texas" and the bombarding of Cherbourgh? It seems they just released the story on that day we went in. The Boston Herald and Globe had a big writeup about the "Texas" and it mentioned where the Barton was hit. But I couldn't get ahold of that clipping and it isn't the one I'm sending. Maybe it was in the Bulletin or Courier.

We've been having a good time on our liberty. I guess you received my card from Revere Beach. Hank, some of the fellows, and I spent a Sunday there. Last week I saw Horace Heidel's Orchestra and a 20-piece girl orchestra. On Thursday our ship had a dance in the John Hancock Hall in Boston and it was really a nice place. They had refreshments, a floor show and an orchestra for dancing. The Captain and his wife were even there.

Have you or the Hartman's heard from Skin lately? I haven't had a letter from him since I was in England. I had letters this week from John, Bernie and George Banyas. Say Pete, haven't you gotten over your "writer's cramp" yet? How is the home team doing? I was sure surprised to hear Jake S. was home. I'll bet Doris is really happy. Wonder if she will get married. Ma did you ever get those pictures back from Faunce's (the ones I took in Bermuda)? Will you send me some when you get them? The snapshot I'm sending was taken by a candid camera man when I was walking down Market St. that day I bought my whites. I just received it last week.

Pete are you still working in Paramount? I guess you'll be going back to school soon or will you? When does football practice start? Ma I could really go for one of your "super duper" dinners right now. I got so used to your cooking while I was home that now I really miss it. Dad don't work too hard on those hot days and take it easy. I've got a sort of another promotion. The Chief made me head man on the auxiliary watch in port. That is, I'm the head of the watch and over three other firemen. At sea, I've got a better watch too, as check man and second to the fellow in charge of watch. Well I have to sign off now folks as I have to do some letter writing. I'll close thinking of you all and send my love.

P.S. Say hello to "Farmer Butz" when he comes home for me.

August 30, 1944
Boston, Mass.

Dear Folks,

I received your letter this week and was very glad to hear from you. The telegram came the next day after I called. But after getting your letter Ma I'm pretty mad. I told you thousands of times if I ever send for or need money to draw it from my account because that's what it's for. Instead you take it from your and Dad's money that you had put away. If I knew you were going to do that I wouldn't have sent for it at all. Why, I'd rather stay on the ship without any money and wait for pay day to come rather than have you do that. So please Ma draw that money from my account that you sent.

Well it's Wednesday and we are still here in dry dock making it just fifty days today. But the chances of getting home this coming weekend are rather slim now. You see ever since Monday they have been rushing the job and the latest "dope" is that we are to leave dry dock tomorrow (Thursday) and be out on sea trials Friday. Now whether we will be in over Saturday and Sunday I don't know yet. But I'm sure praying we will be. I'll call you at the end of the week and let you know for sure.

I've been doing pretty well with mail this week. Had letters from you and Dad, Ray Claus, John, Bernie and a card from Aunt Elise. I finally heard from Skin after two months. I take it he's pretty far out from the way he talks and he says it's awfully hot. I sure got a kick about your telling me of your ball playing Dad. Especially those "one-handers" out of the sky. I would sure liked to see you play. Well folks I'll close for now. If you see any of the Hartmans tell them to drop me a line as I haven't heard from them since I returned from leave. Love to you all.

P.S. Don't forget about drawing the money.

September 5, 1944
Boston, Mass.

Dear Folks,

Just a few lines to let you know I'm still in, but in all probability we are to leave Thursday. Until now we haven't heard any rumors as to where we are headed. We have really been in a long time though. It will be an even two months the 9th of this month. Why we've been in long enough for a battleship or cruiser. I've heard that the ship Bud Norwicki is on never came back after the first invasion of Southern France. I suppose he will be home on leave soon. After being over there that long I suppose he will have plenty of time in the yard too.

I'm sorry that I didn't get home this past weekend, but you know it's just one of those things. They would pick Sunday to go out of all days. We went out on Monday again, yesterday and today we loaded stoves, took on ammunition and fueled the ship. They let us off early Saturday and we got free tickets to the A's-Red Sox game at Fenway Park. Boy! that was one swell game, you probably read about it in the paper. Saturday night a couple of the fellows and I saw a good movie and stage show at the RKO in Boston . We saw Belita the skating star, Smiley

Burnett, Gene Autry's pal, and Phil Reagan the movie star in person. Last week Betty Hutton was here.

How is everything at home? Fine I hope. Well Pete & Butz you will be back to the "dear old school days again" soon huh? I hope both of you do as well this year as you did last. I guess you'll be glad to get back because of football and all Pete. Now don't forget and keep me in touch with all the games and see if you can have the Reviews sent again. I hope you make the first team this year. Say Pete will you send me Harry Kirchner's address? I'd like to drop him a line some time. Well Folks I'll close for now and hope this war comes to an end real soon so I'll be home for good. Give my regards to everyone and I send my love to you all.

September 7–Clear and warm. We left the Boston Navy Yard and were underway at 0800. We arrived in Montauk, Long Island at 1700 via Cape Cod canal.

September 8—Clear and cool. Underway at 0700. Operated with a French sub.

September 9–Operated with the sub.

September 10–Operated with the sub.

September 11–Cloudy and cool. Underway at 0645 at 18 knots and believed to be headed for Panama.

September 12–Clear and warm. Headed due south.

September 13–Clear and warm. Received word that a freighter was torpedoed during the night We are proceeding at 27 knots.

September 14–Clear and warm. Arrived on the scene at 1200. A Liberty ship had been torpedoed and lay dead in the water. Two blimps were patrolling overhead and several other destoyers were there. At 1400 we joined them in the hunt the for the sub.

Sept. 14, 1944

Dear Folks,

How is everyone at home? Fine I hope. Is it very hot? I'm just about melting. I'm out again, but can't say where. You probably noticed the change in my fleet P.O. address. From now on use this new address and I suppose I'd get my mail quicker if you sent it by air mail. Maybe I'll see Skin now. I sure hope so.

Well Pete and Butz how are you doing now that you're back in school? Do you like Sister Afra this year Butz? Pete, how's football coming along? Do you think you'll have a good team this year? Remember me to the "Chief". Don't forget and write once in a while and tell me about the games and send a few clippings.

How's everything at work Dad? Have you been playing any more of those "All Star" games lately? Maybe they'll even have a football team at work or you will play basketball at the Turner Hall. I'm sorry I didn't get home for that chicken dinner Mother. I was sure looking forward to it. Maybe they will be full grown by the time I get to eat one now, but maybe I'll be home for good then. You can make all the chicken and chocolate fudge cakes you want because I'll sure eat them. Ma, will you keep sending the Press and maybe a Bulletin once in a while or the Courier? Not every day, but once in a while so I don't forget what they look like.

I'll have to close for now folks and I will write whenever I can. Give my regards to everyone at home. Love to you all.

September 15–Cloudy and rough with hurricane warnings all along the coast. Gave up the chase hunting for a sub and headed for Norfolk to refuel after leaving the coast of the Carolinas. Arrived at Norfolk and sent to Solomons, Maryland in the Chesapeake Bay to ride out the hurricane. It started at noon with high waves, wind and rain coming down horizontally. Wind was estimated at 93 mph. It lasted all afternoon and cleared up at 1700.

September 16–Clear and warm. Left Solomons, Maryland and returned to Norfolk. Refueled and took on some stoves. Left at 1630 and picked up a communications ship. We're taking it to San Diego.

September 17 —Clear and warm. We passed San Salvador during the night. We're now in the Bahamas.

September 18–Clear and warm. It's getting hotter every day. We were off Cuba at 1600. The Communications ship had to stop for four hours due to a steering casualty. The fireroom temperature is now 110 degrees.

September 19–Slightly cloudy and warm. The fireroom temp. is now 134 degrees at night.

September 20–Clear and warm. Land was sighted at 1100. We arrived at the first locks of the Panama Canal at 1400. Clocks were set back one hour. Passed through the Gatun locks, Gatun Lake, San Miguel Locks and Miraflores locks. Arrived at Balboa on the Pacific side at 2200. We tied up to the oil dock and fueled the ship.

September 21–Cloudy and rain. We took over the stoves in the morning. Underway at 1400. We 're now in the Pacific headed for San Diego.

September 21, 1944

Dear Folks,

Just a few lines to let you know I'm OK and feeling fine. It will probably be a while before you receive this letter, but I'll write a couple more in the meantime. I heard that the hurricane along the Jersey coast did quite a bit of damage, especially near Atlantic City. Did Uncle Carl weather the storm? How was it around home? We just missed it luckily. I've acquired quite a tan now and also have a "brush" haircut. Almost all the fellows have one and some had all their hair cut off. It sure feels cool though. How is everything at home? Has it begun to get cold yet? If it has I sure wish I could be there. I haven't received any letters from you yet, but I suppose I'll get alot when I do. Don't forget the Press & Review Mother. Pete don't forget and write and tell me all about football season and the games. How are you doing in school this year Butz? Do you like it?

How's everything at work Dad? Are you playing any ball lately? Don't work too hard. Well Mother I guess the house is pretty quiet now that

Butz is back to school and no more cowboys and Indians running through the house. Ha ha! You certainly must have done alot of preserving according to your letters Ma. Did Dad put any grapes in the barrel?

I wish I were home to help you hang curtains and move the beds and furniture around when you house clean. And beat the rugs, roll them up and wrap them in paper with moth balls. I sure miss all that Ma. Had a letter from John and he said he's finally going to sea and on an LST. Well he put in for it and so he'd better not complain. I guess that breaks he and Bernie up for now. He said they had some good times together down in Florida. I haven't heard from Skin for awhile. I had a letter from Louise Hartman.

Say Dad where did Martin and Marion Fryman move to? They haven't been around Riverside for some time. Maybe you know where they moved to. Well that's all for today folks. I'll write more later. Please excuse the writing because we've been rolling around a little. Give my regards to everyone at home. Love to you all.

September 22–Cloudy and rainy. We're still headed due north with the clocks set back one hour.

September 23–Cloudy and rainy. The air is cool and water is slightly rough.

September 24–Cloudy, rainy and cool.

September 25–Cloudy, cool and rain. Still headed due north.

September 26–Clear and getting warmer. The clocks were set back one hour.

September 27–Clear with a smooth sea.

September 28–Clear and calm.

September 29–Cloudy and cool. Arrived in San Diego at 1430. Tied up at the repair base and fueled the ship.

September 30–Clear and warm. I had a 1330 liberty. I went into San Diego for a few hours, then to National City, Chula Vista, San Ysidro and the Mexican border near Tijiuana.

October 1–Clear and warm. Had 1200 liberty. Went to Los Angeles and Hollywood.

Western Union
October 1, 1944
San Diego, California

Dear Folks. Arrived safely San Diego yesterday. Am well. Don't worry. Regards to everyone. Love Fran.

October 1, 1944
San Diego, California

Dear Folks,

I suppose by now you have received my card and telegrams saying that I arrived here on Friday. Yesterday we received our first mail with the new P.O. address. It just takes about six days from home by air mail. So far I received three letters and one Press. The mail is really catching up with us so maybe I'll be getting more.

This seems to be pretty nice country, sandy and in some parts palm trees. There's a few orange groves, but most of the fruit growing is done farther inland. Last night was my first liberty and we went into town for a few hours and had something to eat. That's when I sent the telegram. Then we fellows decided to go to Mexico. The border is just 16 miles south of here. We started hitch hiking on the main highway and got there at the town this side of the border. But we found we had to have a pass from our commanding officer so we couldn't go into Mexico. In getting there we got all kinds of riders. We even rode in an open truck on a couple of orange crates. A Mexican was driving and took us right to the border. Oh for the life of a sailor, huh? Man! We travel any ole way just to get there.

The people are really helpful and sociable. Hitch hiking is even better than in Jersey. You just put your thumb out and a car stops. Everybody picks you up. One fellow on our ship has a brother in an army camp and he went to see him. They rode him all around the camp in a "jeep" until he found his brother. I read those clippings you sent about the hurricane. Did it do any damage to any of Uncle Joe's cottages? We just missed being out in the middle of it. We were off North Carolina when we got a message to return to Norfolk as we were heading right into it. We pulled into Norfolk at noon with the storm on our tail and anchored in the Chesapeake. At 10 o'clock it broke and the wind was really blowing. The rain wasn't falling slanted, but horizontal. We went through the Panama Canal in 8 hours. That was an experience in itself to see that piece of engineering. But we didn't get any liberty. It took us seven days from the Canal to San Diego. What surprised me the most is that it is really cold out here and they say sunny California. We have to have blankets at night and wear blues on liberty.

I hope this letter finds everyone well and in good health. Say Pete I'm just dying to hear something of the football season at home so how about dropping me a line? I guess that's all for now folks so I'll bring this to an end. I guess we'll try to make Mexico this afternoon. I ought to be able to get some good souvenirs. We were going to try and get to Los Angeles and Hollywood, but won't have time enough to get that far. I'm going to try and get around as much as I can while I'm here. I'll close now, thinking of you all and send my love. Write soon.

October 2–Clear and warm. Underway at 1100 and headed for Pearl Harbor.

October 3–Cloudy and cool with our course due west at 16 knots. Clocks set back one hour. Saw a large school of porpoises about four miles long.

October 3, 1944

Dear Folks,

I received all your letters, Press and Courier. It sure was good to hear about home and to read the town paper again. By now I hope you have received my letters. How is everything at home? Has it started to get cold yet? I suppose the trees are just changing colors huh?

Received your letter Pete and was glad to hear you beat Pitman. Also that you're playing varsity this year. How did you make out this past week? Boy! you had better beat Burlington and Mt. Holly or I'm going to take a razing. Ray Claus and Vince Fryman are sure lucky to be in Philadelphia. Had a letter from Skin and a whole paragraph cut out. I guess he said a little too much. Do you ever see Al anymore? I haven't heard from him since I wrote to him.

They have the World Series on the radio this afternoon and now the Browns are leading 2-0. We heard Great Lakes and Illinois play college football on Saturday. Well folks this is going to turn out to be a short letter as I haven't anything else to talk about right now. But I'll write more later in the week. Love to you all.

October 4–Clocks set back one hour.

October 5–Clear and warm. Clocks set back one hour. Picked up a fellow from a landing craft with appendicitis. The Doctor operated on him in the afternoon.

October 6–Clear and warm.

October 7–Clear and warm. We expect to arrive in Pearl Harbor tomorrow.

October 8–Clear and warm. Arrived in Pearl Harbor at 1100. Very beautiful scenery and light blue water. Moored to a buoy.

October 9–Clear and warm. We changed commanders at a dress inspection. Commander Callahan was transferred and Commander Dexter came aboard.

October 10–Clear and warm. We went along side the destroyer Tendo.

October 10, 1944
Pearl Harbor

Dear Folks,

I received Butz and Mother's letters yesterday and was very glad to hear from you. I received them in five days. I was sorry to hear that you injured your hand Pete. But you know they say you can't keep a good man down. How did you make out against Moorestown? By the way Pete what's your number this year?

You must be working pretty hard cleaning up the back lot Butz. Did you build your club house yet? Do you still keep the old buggy shined up? Boy! Mother, you sure make my mouth water when you were describing that apple pie. I'd sure like to have some of your good baking right now. Especially one of your super chocolate fudge cakes. Mother I wonder if you sent one in a tin if it would be okay. I would really like to taste one again even if it was stale when it got here.

Hello Dad how is everything with you? I guess it won't be long until you are brushing the snow away to get to the garage instead of hoeing in the garden. How is the weather at home? Have you been going to football games? Ma tells me you and Uncle Lawrence were fixing some shingles on the roof. Wish I could have been there to help you.

I just received a letter from Aunt Elise today. She told me all about the damage around Avalon. She also told me she's sending a fruit cake. We'll have a feast as Hank is expecting one too. I had a letter from Bill Seiler a couple weeks ago. Haven't heard from Skin, John or Bernie for some time. You see Ma we are getting air mail which gets here in a few days. I just received the letter you mailed in Bethlehem and it just took four days. I haven't received any papers for some time. How was your trip to Bethlehem? Did you have a nice time?

All the engineers that sleep together in our compartment chipped in and bought an electric phonograph. Now we can have lots of music. Mother I increased my allotment this month to fifty dollars which is to start the 1st of November. You will get the twenty dollar check for Oct. and at the end of Nov. you should get the fifty dollar check.

I've got a couple of polo shirts for you Pete. You know like the one's "Gator" Fryman's brother sent him. And are they loud. Well I guess that's all for now folks so I'll bring this letter to a close. Thinking of you and sending my love.

P.S. Pete I'm returning your clippings.

October 11–Clear and warm. Went on liberty in Honolulu. Saw sights and bought some souvenirs.

October 12–Clear and warm.

October 13–Clear and warm. Went on liberty in Honolulu and Waikiki Beach. Then we went swimming. I tried to ride a surfboard. Saw and visited the Royal Hawaiian Hotel and Diamond Head. Very beautiful mountains, cane fields, palm trees, bluish green water, sandy beaches and coral reefs.

October 14-20–Squadron maneuvers and firing practice.

October 19, 1944

Dear Folks,

I received Mother's letter dated Oct. 14 and Vince's letter dated Oct. 12 this morning. In all I received about five letters and some of the three-cent mail came. But we don't seem to be getting any packages or newspapers. I've only received one Press and one Courier. I suppose they will all come in one bunch. Had a letter from Skin too and for once it didn't have anything cut out.

How is everyone at home? Fine I hope. Is it still pretty chilly? Boy! I could use some of that Jersey weather. I'm sitting here sweating while I write this letter. I can't wait until I receive your cakes and cookies Mother. Lots of the fellows are expecting packages and we're going to have a big feed when they get here. Sure hope you have luck at at the Bingo soon Ma. If Margaret Cahill won it's beginning to get close anyhow. I'm glad to hear you and Dad had a nice trip to Bethlehem. It must have been nice this time of the year.

How is everything with you Dad? Hope you're not working too hard at the factory. Ma tells me you were doing some painting. Wish I could have been there to help you. Are the chickens still laying? I've a pretty dark tan because I've had a chance to do some swimming and surfboard riding lately at one of the world's famous beaches. The water is real salty. You should see the loud swimming trunks I've got.

Sorry to hear about losing those two games Pete. But you can't win them all and anyway they were close scores. Hank and I are anxiously awaiting the results of the Burlington game as we are going to see who is going to be razed. Sure would like to see you play a game this year since you're playing the whole game and Ma tells me you're playing good ball. Keep it up Pete and you'll get your letter. What's your number this year?

Hello Butz did you receive my card? Don't forget to tell Ma to draw that money for you and you can get whatever you want. I meant one of those pennants for you Butz and one for Pete. I just addressed the envelope to Pete. I have another one for you now, but I can't send it because it would disclose where I'm at. I have some other things for you, but I can't send them just now. On Sunday I went to Mass, confession and communion. I was glad I had the opportunity to go as it was the first chance I had since leaving the states.

While at the U.S.O. in Hollywood I saw a couple of stars, Abbott and Costello were supposed to have been there, but Costello had another death in his family and couldn't appear. We tried to see everything we could in the six hours we were there. Well folks I'll close for now and hope I'll hear from you soon again. Love to you all. P.S. Mother will you see if you can get Al's address and send it to me?

October 21–Clear, warm and calm. Commander and staff of Desmond 60 came aboard.

October 22–Clear and warm. Left Pearl Harbor at 1200 with five other destroyers and North Carolina.

October 22, 1944

Dear Folks,

This morning I received five Press's and two letters. Boy! was I happy to get those papers and read the ole town's news. It sure felt good to read about the old place and the fellows, even if some of the issues were from early September. Also about the hurricane and damage it did along the Jersey coast.

Did you read the article in the Sept. 21 issue of the Press (Uniform Jottings) about Jack Getz? If you didn't see it you should look it up. I heard Hank had a letter and he told me that his sister wrote and told him that Riverside lost the Bristol game. Boy! Pete the team sure must be having the tough breaks. Am I taking a razing! Hank said Burlington beat Moorestown 25-0 and Moorestown beat Riverside. So he claims Burlington will roll over Riverside. You just run up the score against them Pete.

Well folks I guess that's all for now as the lights are about to go out. I'll close hoping that all of you are fine and in good health. Love to you all.

P.S. I'm sending some clippings from the paper that you can save for me.

October 24–Clear and warm. Practiced firing. We heard a news broadcast saying that a big sea battle is taking place in the Philippines.

October 28–Clear and hot. Crossed the International Dateline at 180 degrees meridian and moved one day ahead. The temperature now averaging 103–105 degrees.

October 29–Clear and hot. We fueled the ship from the North Carolina.

October 30–Clear and warm.

October 30, 1944

Dear Folks,

Hello everyone, how are things at home? Have you had any snow to shovel as yet? I suppose it must be pretty chilly by now. I'm O.K. and feeling fine. Still getting lots of sun tan every day. Pretty soon I'll be looking like "Ebony" White on C.R. Taylor. This sure is nice weather, but you sweat all the time. We had a pretty good feed on Navy Day–chicken, cigars and all, but it couldn't compare with your cooking Ma.

How are the games going Pete? Has your luck changed any? Sure hope you get your letter. Is the Chief still in 22H? Tell him I was asking about him. Hello Butz how's your school days coming along? Are you still getting those good marks and keeping the "green beetle" all shined up?

Well Dad how is everything with you? When are you going to write one of those "rainy day" letters? Ha! Ha! Hello Mother, did you hit that bingo yet? I received about four or five Press's and the Bulletin. Hank received two of his Christmas fruit cakes already so I suppose I'll be getting mine pretty soon. Boy! we'll really have a feast. Have you heard from John yet? Send his address if you get it.

Well folks I'll have to be closing for now. Give my regards to everyone at home as I can't write to them all. Love to you all.

October 31–Clear and hot. We arrived at Eniwetok in the Marshall Islands and fueled the ship from the tanker.

November 1–Left Eniwetok at 0700 with the North Carolina. We are supposed to be going to the Admiralty Islands.

November 2–Slightly cloudy. Now only 40 miles and 35 minutes from the equator. Ceremonies for entering the Davey Jones domain were being conducted when the ship was ordered to change course and proceed to the Ulithi Atoll instead of the Admiralty Islands.

November 3–Clear and warm.

November 3, 1944

Dear Folks,

Just a few lines to let you know that I'm OK and feeling fine and getting tanner every day as I'm getting plenty of sunlight. Sure could use some of that November weather in Jersey. How is everyone at home? Fine I hope. Have you had any blizzards yet? I guess the only snow I'll be seeing will be in pictures. How does Riverside look now? It must be pretty deserted.

Well Pete how is the team doing? Have you won any games yet? Ha! Ha! Just kidding. Boy! if you don't beat Burlington and Mt. Holly I'll never live it down. Are you still playing first string? I guess it won't be long before you will meet Palmyra. How does it feel to be a junior this year? Tell the Chief I was asking about him when you see him.

Hank and I were just talking about the good times we are going to have when we get home for good. He sleeps right under me and we're always looking for fun. We engineers have our own phonograph and are always trying to jitterbug among ourselves. Boy! what a crazy bunch. We sure have some good times.

We haven't received mail for some time now as we've been out. But when we do maybe I'll get the packages and rest of the Press's you sent. I only wish you could send one of your swell dinners Mother, but when I come home for good you can cook anything and I'll eat it all. I'm certainly not picky like I used to be a couple of years ago. Have you heard from Skin or John lately ? Haven't heard a word from John since he left Florida. I wonder what's the matter with the Hartmans. I only had one letter since we left Boston.

Well folks there's not much to write about out here so I'll have to sign off for now. Hope to hear from you real soon. Give my regards to everyone. Love to you all.

November 4–Clear and warm.

November 4, 1944

Dear Folks,

Here's just a few more lines to let you know that I'm well and feeling fine. How is everyone at home? Have you finished your preserving yet? Boy! I wish that I could be home to sample some of your good cooking. I suppose all of you are wearing coats and mufflers by now if I know that Jersey weather. We heard that it snowed in New York already.

Just now they started to play "Dear Mom" on the phonograph and it sure makes me think of you Ma and makes me kinda homesick. But Ma this can't last much longer and then I'll be home for good. In fact, Hank and some of the other "east coasters" and I said that we won't wait for any slow moving trains. We'll buy a jeep and pile in and head straight for Jersey. I guess you wonder why I'm just writing to you today Mother. Well I just wanted to tell you to buy Dad's, Pete's, Butz's and your own Christmas presents for me.

My November check is supposed to come through this month for $50 so will you pick out a nice present for Dad, Vince and Butz and then you can buy your own Mother or keep the money. Whatever you wish. Please don't forget and do this Ma or I'll be disappointed. Maybe you can write and let me know what you bought them so it will kinda seem as though I was there to give them to you. Don't forget your own present Ma and make it a really nice one. Don't forget now.

I sure hope this will be the last time that I'll be away. The next time we'll all celebrate together. And how!! Well Mother, I'll have to close for now as its almost time for chow. Sending you loads of love and thinking of you always.

November 5–Arrived at the Ulithi Atoll in the Caroline Islands at 0600. Took on ammunition and stoves and left at 1600.

November 6–Clear and warm.

November 7–Fueled the ship at sea from the tanker.

November 8–Now screening for a large task force of carriers and battleships. Rough weather. We're now approximately 500 miles off the central Philippines and supporting the air strike against Manila.

November 9–Clear and warm.

November 10–Clear and warm.

November 11–Now 80 miles off Luzon. Planes bombed Manila in the morning. We went to battle stations twice this morning due to Jap aircraft.

November 12–Fueled the ship.

November 13–Clear and warm with seas slightly rough. Now approximately 40 miles off Luzon. Planes took off to bomb Manila and Leyte. Went to General Quarters twice again for enemy aircraft. In the afternoon, "Duke" Baron was lost over the side and drowned.

November 14–Clear and warm. Services were held for "Duke" Baron at 1115 with burial at sea. Planes again went inland to bomb.

November 15–Now back in the fueling zone.

November 15, 1944

Dear Folks,

Hello! everyone. Just a few words to let you know that I'm fine and feeling O.K. Hope all of you at home are the same. I haven't had a chance to do any letter writing or receive any mail for a couple of weeks as we have been pretty "occupied" lately.

How is the weather at home? Had any snowfall yet? If not, I'll bet the weather is pretty cold. Did you have your sled out yet Butz? I guess it seems funny to you to be saying this, but it's so hot and we sweat so much we have to take salt pills.

How is the football team doing Pete? I suppose it won't be long and you'll be playing Palmyra. Sure hope you win and get your letter. Hello Butz, how are you doing at school? Have you got your Christmas list already for Santa Claus? Are you done with your house cleaning yet Mother? Sure wish I could be there to help you with it. Haven't received any packages or papers let alone mail yet Ma. I found out from the pay-master that my $50 allotment won't go through until December. The time sure goes fast out here and we save money anyway. Just use enough to buy soap and toilet articles.

Hello Dad how are you doing? Is the "gas buggy" still running in the cold weather? Well folks I'll have to close this letter so that I can get it in for censoring. Give my regards to everyone as this is the only letter I'll have time to write. I close thinking of you all and send all my love.

November 16–Clear and warm. Fueled from the tanker.

November 17 —Clear and warm.

November 18–Overcast and warm. The Captain spoke tonight telling us we are heading for Luzon and expect to be about 100 miles from there by morning. The planes from all of the carriers are going to bomb Manila and Luzon.

November 19–Clear and warm. The carriers sent up planes about 0700. G.Q. called at 1800. Jap bombers attacked the task force and dropped bombs just missing the carriers. It was reported 15 Jap planes were shot down by our fighters.

November 20–Rough and windy. Hear we are to return to Ulithi.

November 20, 1944

Dear Folks,

How is everyone and everything back in Riverside and good ole Jersey? I sure would like to be there watching a football game and getting half frozen. As it is I'm sitting here writing with my shirt off and sweating. Have you had any snowfall yet? I guess Butz is getting his sled already to go huh?

I'm O.K. and feeling fine although I could sure use some of your good cooking Ma. Powdered milk, powdered eggs and dehydrated potatoes could never compare with your cooking. Sure could use one of Uncle Carl's cows. Next time I get the chance I'm going to drink fresh milk until it runs out of my ears ha! ha!

I haven't received any mail since Nov. 1. But we hear we are to receive some in the next couple of days. So maybe I'll get alot then. Out here the only time we get mail is when a ship comes along and transfers a bag to us.

Have you heard from John or Skin lately? I haven't heard from John since he was in Florida. Is Lester Yearly still in Italy? Well Pete I guess your big game is coming up this week huh? Sure hope you beat them. How did you do against Mt. Holly and Burlington? Is the school having any dances this year? Well folks since I've just written you a letter the other day I've run out of words already. Until I can write some more I'll close. Give my regards to everyone. Love to you all.

November 21–Clear and warm. Now headed to Ulithi. Carrier planes bombed the Jap Islands on the way back.

November 22–Clear, warm and calm. Arrived at Ulithi. We fueled the ship from the tanker and received mail.

November 23-26–Tied alongside the Destroyer Tendo Dixie for repairs.

Thanksgiving Day
November 23, 1944

Dear Folks,

I hit the jackpot today and received ten letters. Five of them were from home, all dated from October 30 to November 9. I also heard from Bernie, Skin and a couple from the feminine population! Ha! Ha! This is the first real bunch of mail we got in a couple of weeks. Just now I'm in the mess hall answering my mail. It looks like a library with all the tables filled with fellows writing. Well today was Thanksgiving and yet it didn't seem much like Thanksgiving in that the weather was much different from a typical Thanksgiving. Instead of going to a football game in the morning and getting half-frozen then coming home and eat dinner, we just about melted to death from the heat. It's one of the hottest days I've seen yet. I spent most of the day working on a valve in the fireroom, drinking water and eating salt pills. Well anyway, one consolation was that we received mail and that really boosted up our morale 100%. Oh yes, I almost forgot, I received the first of my packages, a fruit cake from Aunt Elise. I'm going to drop her a line and thank her the first chance I get. I'm still looking forward to that cake though Mother. I just can see it now, mmmm!!! At least getting that package shows they are coming through anyway.

We had a pretty good dinner–turkey, potatoes, carrots & peas, cranberry sauce, apple pie, olives, ice cream, peanuts and a cigar. Guess what we had for supper? Stew. A big let down, but that dinner still couldn't compare with one of yours Mother.

Well that's enough about me–How is everyone at home? Did you spend a cold Thanksgiving or was it nice out? Boy! I hope you beat them Pete. I guess I'm pretty well informed on the football dope after getting all those letters. Received your typewritten letter too Pete. You did all right. I showed it to Hank and he didn't have much to razz me about after reading your description of the game. I didn't tell him about that illegal player deal though. Sure glad you beat Mt. Holly. I'll have something to razz Carolyn about now. She was so sure "Holly" would win. Carolyn—(just one of the girls Ha! Ha!). Sorry about your having all those injuries Pete, but I guess they can't keep a good man down. Everyone at home writes and tells me how good you are. I'm proud of you Pete for playing varsity this year and getting your letter. I suppose almost everyone on the ship knows that my brother is playing varsity football.

Had a letter from Skin and he seems to be OK, but I haven't figured out yet where he's at. Do his folks know yet? Bernie's back in Vero Beach, Florida. He told me that John is still in Fort Pierce and waiting for his orders. Maybe that's why more of us are hearing from him. He's probably afraid to write after telling everyone he was going on an LST and to sea. So George Banyas and Ray Claus were home on leave–I'll bet they had a good time together. Have you seen anyone else around town that I know? So Butz I'll bet you were glad to have off from school on Thanksgiving. Did you go to the game? When are you going to write me another letter?

Say Dad, Mother tells me you have turned from "ballplayer" to a "poet". I'll bet you really have them roaring in the shop. I can just see you now. When are you going to drop me a line and tell me about it?

I'm glad you and Dad had a nice time at the ice-capades Mother. I never had a chance to see them, but I did see the roller varsities when we were in Boston. It was just like the ice capades, but on roller-skates. Let me know if and when my new allotment comes through with you Ma. It is supposed to go into effect in December and don't forget to take care of my Christmas shopping for me like I told you in one of my previous letters Mother.

Boy! I guess you were surprised when you read about Jim's old ship. We probably knew it before you. Had a letter from Johnny Getz and he's moved again. Boy! they're always moving him somewhere. He said he visited his Uncle Arthur. I guess it was the first time he saw him in some time. He sure was surprised.

Well folks, I suppose you're surprised at the length of this letter. Our getting mail today gave me something to talk about. I'll close for now (better before I run out of ink) and send all of you my love. Give my regards to everyone back home.

November 26–Clear, warm and calm. Went ashore on Magmog Island today for a beer party. Four cans per man. There's nothing here but sand and palm trees.

November 27–Clear and warm. Left Ulithi about 0630 with most of a squadron (6) of destroyers.

November 28 —Clear and hot, temperature about 108. Held squadron maneuvers and firing.

November 29–Clear and warm with a slight rain. Beautiful day, very calm. We are supposed to arrive at Leyte, Phillipine Islands today. Went to G.Q. at 0300. Main battery fired at a Jap patrol plane. At 0745 another Jap plane was sighted. Land sighted at 0800. Anchored off Leyte at 1200. All kinds of ships are present. At 1300 a Philippines outrigger canoe came alongside us and traded Jap money for clothing. They said they took the money from dead Japs on the beach. The two young boys who were in the boat said the Japs took all their clothes and burned their belongings. Went to G.Q. at 2000–condition "Red". Beautiful full moon.

LCI's laid a smoke screen to cover the ships. At 2100 we got underway due to an air attack.

November 30–Cloudy and cool with rain showers. Joined the 7th fleet today. Battleships–West Virginia, New Mexico, Maryland and Colorado. Cruisers–Portland, Minneapolis, Phoenix, Denver, Columbia and Montpelier. We fueled off the New Mexico around 1000. G.Q. at 1300 and 2030.

December 1–Cloudy and cool with rain. Went to G.Q. three times today.

December 1, 1944

Dear Folks,

Here I am again with a few lines to let you know that I'm O.K., well and feeling fine. I hope this letter finds all of you at home the same and in good health. I imagine by now the weather must be pretty "cool" ha! ha! Boy! are we having a hot winter. This is about the hottest December I ever spent. One day the temperature hit 108 degrees. If the temperature falls to around 98 degrees we usually put on jackets ha! ha!

Not much more news since my last letter except that we had a beer party last night. We went ashore on an island and were allowed 3 cans per man. So you can see that there wasn't any danger of anyone getting drunk. We had a good time though. How is the weather now? I suppose you already have the storm windows up. Boy! I can hear them banging up in the back room now. Did you get to shovel any snow yet Butz?

I'm still anxiously awaiting the results of the Riverside game. We haven't received any mail for a couple of weeks now. I've acquired lots of souvenirs but can't mail them due to censorship regulations. Well Pete, now that the football season is just about over are you going in for basketball or are you going to recuperate from the football season? Ma told me you sure got some bad knocks.

Hello Butz, when are you going to drop me a line? I guess you can't wait for the holidays to come huh? How's "Spottie" doing? Well Mother I guess the December weather keeps you busy during the day running up and down putting coal on the fire. Haven't received any other packages yet, other than Aunt Elise's. Boy! that fruit cake didn't last long. I guess we split that between seven or eight fellows.

Say Dad when are you going to write one of your annual letters? I'll bet you have trouble getting the "green beetle" started in the mornings now huh–well when the war is over and I get home we'll really get a "good car". I'll have to close as its getting late. Give my regards to everyone at home. Love to you all.

December 2–Rainy and warm. We're still in the harbor moored by a communication ship. Went to G.Q. about 5 times. Went alongside the supply ship for stoves in the afternoon.

December 3–Rainy and cool. We're still anchored off Leyte. The outriggers are still coming out to the ship. Went to G.Q. twice.

December 4–Overcast and cool.

December 5–Clear and warm. Went to G.Q. at 0400. Beautiful moonlit nights. LCI's made a smoke screen to cover the ships. We are supposed to get underway tomorrow.

December 6–Cloudy, warm and calm. At 1000 Major General Chamberlain, one of MacArthur's staff officers, and two war correspondents came aboard. Underway at 1130. We are escorting an amphibious force consisting of LPD's, LCI's, LST's and minesweepers. The captain spoke over the PA system this afternoon and said we are to make a landing tomorrow morning in Orinoc Bay, about 7 miles below the town of Orinoc and on the west side of Leyte. He said we are to expect enemy resistance.

December 7 (Pearl Harbor Day)–G.Q. called at 0200. We are now in the bay with land visible at 1 mile on either side of us. Large mountains in the distance with palm branches along the water. All hands called to battle stations at 0530. It's cloudy and getting daylight. Bombardment of the beach started at 0643. At 0650, troops started ashore in barges and met some return fire from the shore with shells falling as close as 100 yards. P-38's were overhead for air cover. 3 Jap planes dove on an LPD in a suicide dive. Two of them hit the water and another crashed into it setting it on fire. It later had to be sunk by shell fire from the O'Brien. P-38's were in a dog fight with Zeros and shot down two. Battle stations called again at 1300 with Jap planes overhead. A plane started in to drop bombs and was shot down by all the ships firing at it. At 1330 a Jap "Berty" tried a suicide dive on our ship. It came in aft coming forward. Everything opened up on him and was shot down just missing the bridge and crashed into the water about 50 yards over our bow. We started retiring about 1500. Jap planes still overhead. Two more Jap suicide planes crashed into an LPD and a destroyer at 1630. We secured from G.Q. at 2030 after being at battle stations for 24 hours.

December 8–Cloudy, rainy and calm. Went to G.Q. at 0700. Arrived back in San Pedro Bay on the east side of Leyte at 0800. Went to G.Q. again at 0900. We are moored near the hospital ship Mercy which took battle casualties aboard. Went alongside a tanker to fuel at 1300. Came alongside of an ammunition ship to take off ammo at 1530. Anchored at 2000. It's still raining.

December 9–Rainy, cloudy and cool. Anchored off a communications ship.

December 10–Cloudy and cool. Went to G.Q. twice. Still at anchor.

December 11–Clear and cool. Underway at 0600. Went alongside a tanker to fuel. In the afternoon I volunteered to go with a working party into Taipan on Leyte Gulf for mail. We left the ship in a Higgins boat and it took us about two hours to reach the shore. On the way in we passed the air field and saw a dead Jap lying on the beach. When we landed at the beach we found a mass of gooey, soupy, smelling mud as we were in the middle of the rainy season in the Philippines. We walked to the shed they called a post office, knee deep in mud. There were trucks and all kinds of equipment everywhere. There were about 300 bags of mail, but none for our ship. We arrived back at the ship at 0530 all wet, covered with mud and no mail. Jap planes came in after dark and bombed the beach. They hit an oil tanker and a destroyer off shore.

December 12–Clear, warm and calm. We went to quarters for a message at 0830 and the captain spoke to us on the fantail. He told us we are going to make a landing on the island of Mindanao about 130 miles from Manila. We are to expect enemy resistance in planes, subs and PT boats. Underway at 1430 with 3 cruisers, the Phoenix Nashville and Boise. Went to G.Q. at 1800. Jap planes reported in the vicinity.

December 13–Clear, warm and calm. Routine G.Q. at 0600. We joined the rest of the task force, including PT boats, LCI's, LST's, LPD's, destroyers, cruisers, battleships and carriers. G.Q. at 0830 fired 5 inch at a Jap reconnaissance plane. G.Q. at 1130 as enemy planes reported in the vicinity. G.Q. sounded at 1530, saw a "kamikaze" suicide plane crash into the bridge of the cruiser Nashville who had been cruising on our starboard side of the convoy. G..Q. at 1800 with planes reported approaching on our port beam. A P-38 shot one down over us. A twin engine bomber dove on us and all of the convoy fired, but he was knocked down by a P-47. A P-47 shot another down just ahead of us. Bill Reilly and myself went up with Repair II to help carry 40 MM ammo to the gunners at sunset. Another bomber came over us and the whole convoy fired chasing him over the horizon. Secured from G.Q. at 2000.

December 14 —Clear, hot and calm. Yesterday our position was off the Island of Negros heading due south. Today at 1400 we are off the island of Panay heading due north. Routine G.Q. at 0630. Went to G.Q. again at 1100. Planes reported 30-35 miles in front of us. G.Q. again at 1300 as some ships in the rear of the convoy fired 5" guns at the planes.

December 15–Clear and calm with a glass sea. G.Q. at 0500. At 0527 we opened fire broadsides on a Jap surface craft. It turned out to be a small tanker which caught fire and sank. At 0600, the landings started with the troops meeting bitter resistance. Our squadron is operating with the Phoenix, Portland and Boise as an anti-aircraft screen off shore. At 0830 a radar contact was reported on enemy planes. We now are approximately ½ mile off shore patrolling the shore line. This country is very rugged with big mountains. An LST and LPD were hit and burning off shore. Most of the troops had landed by 1200. G.Q. at 1300, a crippled Jap destroyer reported on the other side of the island. The Walke, a destroyer in our squadron, went in to sink it. At 1400 Jap planes appeared near our beach and engaged in a dog fight with Corsairs who shot them down. G.Q went at 1500, 1515 and 1535 having radar contact on enemy planes, but none sighted At 1930 I was on deck and all ships opened fire on an enemy plane in the darkness overhead. AA fire from one of the carriers on our port side brought it down, hitting the water and burning brightly. We secured from battle stations at 2000 after being on stations for 24 hours straight. Boy! am I tired! It was a very beautiful sunset tonight, one of the nicest I've seen. The sea is as calm as glass.

December 16–Cloudy and cool with a choppy sea. G.Q. sounded at 0200. We had radar contact on the planes. We left Mindanao at 0800, making 29 knots to catch a convoy going to Leyte. Put four boilers online at 0930. Caught up to the convoy at 1230 and slowed to 11 knots. G.Q. at 1900 for sunset General Quarters. Now headed back to Leyte. 9 days until Christmas.

December 17–Cloudy, cool and choppy. Speeded up to 25 knots and reached Leyte at 1000. Went along a tanker to fuel. Took on ammunition in the afternoon. Anchored about ½ mile off beach.

December 18–Clear, cool and calm. G.Q. at 0900–Air Raid.

December 18, 1944

Dear Folks,

This is my first opportunity in quite some time to do any writing as we have been pretty "busy" lately. Today was the first time we received mail since Thanksgiving and I received one from Pete dated Nov. 13 and one from Dad dated Nov. 16. I don't believe I was ever so glad to receive mail in all of my life. Altogether I received seven letters and a Christmas card. The latest letter was postmarked Nov. 29.

Thanks for your long letter Dad, I knew you would get around to writing. I was glad to hear that you are doing new work and that it is alot easier. So far Mother I haven't received any other packages other than the one fruit cake I got from Aunt Elise on Thanksgiving. Mother, in Pete's letter he said something about your being sick in bed.I do hope you're up and feeling well again.

Sure glad to hear that you finished up the season by beating Palymyra Pete. I'll bet you really celebrated that night. I'll send those shirts I told you about as soon as I get the chance. I also have some for Butz. Glad to hear that Pat Hovan was home. I haven't seen him in some time. Also, that you have seen Paul Isenberg. I had letters from Skin, Al Russo and Ray Clauss. I haven't run into Skin yet, but if we ever see each other we'll have alot to talk about.

How is everything at home? Has is snowed yet? Say Butz when are you going to drop me a line? Haven't heard from you in a long time. Are you still prepping the "buggy" running? Well folks I'll have to make this letter rather short and close for now as its getting late. I'll write tomorrow. Give my regards to everyone at home and tell them I was thinking about them . Love to you all.

December 19–Clear, warm and calm. We're still at the same anchorage. Received our first mail today since we arrived in the Philippines.

December 19, 1944

Dear Folks,

Just a few more lines to let you know that I'm OK and feeling fine. This is sort of a continuation from yesterday's letter which I ended so abruptly. It is only six days before Christmas and how time flies. It was just two years ago yesterday that I went on the old Simpson. On Jan. 7 it will make 27 months that I've been in. Boy! it seems like just last year. Here I was only a kid just turned seventeen and now I'll be twenty. I've sure learned alot and seen a lot in that time and I'll be able to talk about it for years to come.

It will hardly seem like Christmas out here as all we see is sky and water and haven't a chance to look at newspapers or see Christmas trees. The weather isn't appropriate and hardly seems like the Christmas season. But I'm thankful for alot of things and that I'm alive and well. I know lots of fellows worse off than I am. After all this, we fellows will really appreciate home and maybe it won't be long until we're home for good and all be together for next Christmas.

Mother have you received my new allotment yet? I believe it has started already as I've noticed it in my pay as I'm getting less now. This is a good place to save money as all we need to buy are things at the ship store like toilet articles, tobacco, candy or stationary. I very seldom spend more that five dollars a month. I already have over a hundred on the books and when I get over one hundred fifty I'm going to start sending it home. But we can only send $100 and up at a time.

I hope everyone at home is all right and well. In your letter of Nov. 16 you said it hadn't snowed yet. I suppose it's slow coming this year, but I guess you'll have lots of it when it comes. Has there been any ice skating yet? We fellows really have a good time although we're way out here. We pass the time by reading books from the ship's library, playing pinochle, playing our jitterbug records or playing jokes on one another. There's a fellow from Akron that jokes with Hank and I. Boy! is he fun. He's about twice the size of Bill Reese. Almost every watch I stand I wind up by having salt pills put in my coffee.

Hank and I often talk about Burlington and Riverside and what we're going to do when we get home again. There's also two fellows from Haddon Heights and one from Florence. He took a razing from me about losing to Riverside. He looks alot like Phil Isden that lives next door to us. Well folks I'll close for now. Give my Christmas greetings to everyone at home because I don't have time to write to everyone. I sent cards to everyone I could. I close thinking of you and sending my love.

December 20 —Clear, warm and calm. Still at anchor. We heard today that we may possibly be in port for Christmas. That's something to be thankful for. Clear night with ¾ moon.

December 21–Clear, hot and calm. At anchor. Regular "turns too" in the fireroom. Last night we went to G.Q. with Jap planes overhead. Ships in the harbor fired and shot down one plane.

December 22–Cloudy, hot and calm. At anchor. Had below deck inspection by the Captain today. G.Q. sounded right in the middle of a movie at 1900. Clear moonlit night.

December 23–Clear, awfully hot and calm. This is going to be a hot Christmas, the temperature now is 105 degrees. Personnel inspection today by the Captain. Had some Philippine bananas from the natives that came alongside in an outrigger canoe. They were small and tasted like strawberries. G.Q. at 1630 –Air Alert.

December 24–Clear, warm and hot. Went to Mass on the Phoenix at 1000. I was going to midnight mass, but we had an air raid at 2300 and shore AA batteries fired at planes. Played Christmas carols on the phonograph at midnight.

December 24, 1944

Dear Folks,

A few lines to let you know that I'm well and feeling fine. Also to wish all of you back home a very "Merry Christmas". Out here we haven't any Christmas trees to look at and the weather is roasting hot, but we still have the Christmas spirit. We are thankful that we are alive and well and to be in port for Christmas. This morning I heard mass on another ship where they had their own chaplain. It was a very nice service and the priest had a swell sermon about Christmas and why we should be thankful even though we aren't able to be home for Christmas.

Tomorrow we are supposed to have a big dinner with entertainment in the afternoon. There's going to be some boxing matches, a fishing contest and alot of fellows are going to sing and play different instruments. After that, we're all going to sing Christmas carols. It's also rumored that we may have some beer. We have some more new records for our phonograph and some nice Christmas carols. So in all, we will have a Christmas even without a tree.

According to today's news you people at home must be having an exceptionally cold Christmas. The news said that most of the northeastern states are having below zero weather and that New Jersey had a low of 34 below and New York and Pennsylvania 13 below. Is that true? It must be something like the blizzard of "88" at home. I can't ever remember it ever being that cold. If that's the case maybe it's a good thing I'm in this heat. Well folks I'll have to close for now as "chow" is going down. Write soon and love to all of you.

December 25–Christmas Day. Clear, hot and calm. Had movies in the mess hall in the morning. Had a big Christmas dinner and entertainment in the afternoon. G.Q. sounded at 1800–Air Alert.

December 26–Clear, warm and cooler.

December 27–Clear, warm and cooler.

December 28–Cloudy and calm. We fueled the ship from a tanker and loaded stoves.

December 29–Cloudy, cool and calm.

December 30–Clear, cool and calm. Regular "turns too" today.

December 30, 1944

Dear Folks,

How is everyone at home? Fine and in good health I hope. How did you spend the holidays? I'll bet you had a "White Christmas" at home. We heard that all the N.E. states had snow and temperatures as low as 25 and 30 below zero. Boy! could we have used some of that weather. Christmas week out here was as hot as it has ever been.

Our Christmas turned out to be a rather enjoyable one after all. We spent it in port with a good dinner and entertainment. The following was our dinner menu: tomato juice cocktail; roast turkey; sliced ham;

giblet gravy; cranberry sauce; mashed sweet potatoes; buttered peas; carrots; nuts; ice cream; lemonade; candy; cigars and cigarettes. Sounds good huh? I think this was about the best holiday dinner I had aboard ship. In all, it was a swell feed, but could never compare with your home cooked dinners Mother. And I mean it–I'll prove it to you Ma when I come home by eating everything except beans and rice (ugh).

I went to church in the morning on another ship and during dinner we had Christmas music on the radio coming from the states. After dinner, some of the fellows put on a comedy act, sang songs and carols, told jokes, etc. On Christmas Eve we started up our ole phonograph and played Christmas carols for about an hour. We wound up by playing "Basin Street Blues" and the "Two O'Clock Jump". To make the Christmas week complete I received about seven letters and six cards. Haven't received any packages since Aunt Elise's first cake on Thanksgiving and only two papers. But I guess we'll receive them eventually. My mouth is watering waiting to receive that chocolate cake Ma. Just to show you how our mail is delayed sometimes I received a couple of letters today from Oct. 25th. Received one of your super duper letters Dad and I had a good laugh. Especially where you told me about your poems. Boy! that was sure good. I even showed it to a couple of the fellows and had them laughing. Also received a letter from Jim Anderson, it was nice of him to drop a line.

So Skin's in Florida Island. I was about going crazy trying to figure out where he was. I looked on a map and it's in the Solomon Islands near Guadalcanal. I sure hope we run into each other some time. Maybe I'll run into Al Russo out here. Glad to hear John Wilkerson was home. Had a card from Bernie saying he got a leave for Christmas. Well Pete what are you doing with yourself now that the football season is over? I'll bet you still are celebrating that victory over Palmyra. Are you playing any basketball? Did you get any ice skating in yet?

Hello Butz, how do you like the winter weather? Did you do any sledding yet? How was "Santa Claus" to you? Thanks for your nice card and letter. Say Butz when I get home and get my car I'll let you clean it all the time for me. How will that be? Hello Mother, I haven't received any letters from you lately. I hope you aren't sick or anything. In one of Pete's letters he said that you were in bed with a little grippe. I do hope you were up and well for Christmas. Don't be working so hard Ma and take it easy. Don't worry about me Ma as I'm fine and well. I'll never have to worry with all your prayers for me.

You should hear the quartet the fellows have. We beat out a couple of numbers like "You Are My Sunshine", "Ole Mill Stream" and "Home on the Range" etc. I guess in all it sounds like a hog calling contest with all contestants turning up at once. Ha! Ha! In Dad's letter he said that my $50 allotment came through. So now Mother you can take out as much as you need each month and bank the rest for me. Now don't forget Ma.

Hi! Dad, how's the poet? Have you been up to your tricks lately? I'm still laughing about Ma putting that tooth paste on your neck. Have you been up to the Pines lately? Did Uncle Lawrence go deer hunting this year? Well folks I guess its about time I brought this letter to a close as I'm getting sleepy. So I'll say so long for now and a "Happy New Year" to you all. Give my regards to everyone at home. Love to you all.

December 31—Clear, warm and calm. Mail and Christmas packages arrived. Topped off fuel from the ship and loaded stoves. I had the 8-12 auxiliary watch. Woke all the fellows in the compartment at mid-night to wish everyone a "Happy New Year".

December 31, 1944

Dear Mother, Dad, Pete & Butz,

Well folks, here it is the last day of ole "44" and tomorrow it will be the new "45". So first of all I want to wish you a very "Happy New Year".

I only wish I could be there to celebrate it with you. But this is the beginning of a new year and I sincerely hope that this one will end all the skirmish and bring us back again for good.

Boy! folks I was sure happy today–Guess what? My packages came. Yes they arrived on New Years Day. Today, 39 bags of mail and packages came aboard. So far I received three from home and one from the Hartmans. As I write they still have about ten bags to sort yet. It seems as though all of it is catching up to us at once. The mail clerk is really kept busy this week.

I want to thank you alot for the packages and gifts. They were really swell– they all arrived just as you sent them with not a thing smashed or broken. The only thing was the fudge which just started to get mildew. Several of the fellows packages were all smashed and broken and some were all crumbs and undistinguishable. A couple of them remarked to me how intact mine were and well wrapped. After I opened them I saw the medals inside. That must have really helped Mother.

Each box was packed so nice and each little gift wrapped separate. Maybe it wasn't good to see and smell that Christmas tree. I've got some of it on a red ribbon hanging over my bunk. One fellow above us received a little artificial tree and he has it hanging up. I can use everything you sent, socks, handkerchiefs, soap, toothbrushes. As for the cookies and goodies, you should see me dive into them. It was sure good to get something like that after eating beans and rice.

Jan. 1, 1945

Had to continue this letter today as it was time to go on watch last night. We really put on the "feed bag" last night staying up most of the night eating cookies, candy, fruit cake and making coffee. You should have seen us when twelve o'clock came. We were aboard ship, but it sure sounded like New Years Eve. A couple of the fellows and I rigged up a bunch of noise makers and then went around waking up everybody and hollering "Happy New Year". Then we put on a swing record on our phonograph and that made it louder yet. It's a wonder that you couldn't hear us way back in the states. Did you spend New Years at home or at the Andersons?

Today they're still sorting packages. I'm waiting to see if the chocolate cakes arrive in as good a condition as the packages. We had a good New Years dinner with turkey, potatoes, bread filling, vegetables, cake, ice cream, lemonade, nuts and candy. I guess that's all for now folks. I want to thank you again for all the swell things. By the look of my locker I suppose I'll be eating for weeks to come. So long for now, I close thinking of you and send all my love.

1945

January 1–Monday–Clear, warm and calm. Still at anchor off Leyte Island. Commanders came aboard for a conference.

January 2–Clear, warm and calm–another conference today. Captain Dexter talked to the crew at 1500 and told us we are to get underway at 2200 with the battleships and cruisers and are going to Manila Bay where the troops are going to land on Luzon. We are to go in with the minesweepers, and sweep the bay for 3 days and nights. Then amphibious forces are to land. Underway at 2200.

January 3–Clear and warm with a glassy sea. The task force is now forming with battleships, cruisers, flat tops, destroyers, several Australian destroyers and cruisers. We are heading north through Mindanao. We started at 15 knots. G.Q. at 1900. A Jap bomber dropped bombs missing an Australian cruiser by 100 yards. Our ship fired at the plane. Secured from G.Q. at 1945. Beautiful full moon tonight and very beautiful sunset. We are supposed to arrive in Manila Bay tomorrow night.

January 4–Clear and warm with a glassy sea. Dawn G.Q. at 0600. G.Q. at 0830 with radar contact. G.Q. at 1130 with radar contact on the planes. G.Q. at 1800, fired at Jap bombers overhead and dove into a carrier which later had to be sunk. The survivors were picked up by a destroyer. Moonlit night. At 2400 we were off Mindanao Island and saw a ship burning on the beach.

January 5–Clear, calm and warm. Dawn G.Q. at 0600. Went to G.Q. at 0830. We had radar contact on enemy planes and were at G.Q. until 1500. We are now only 60 miles from Lingayen Gulf. Our planes sighted two Jap destroyers 40 miles away–sank one and damaged the other. Went to G.Q. at 1800. Jap suicide planes dove and hit a carrier, cruiser and destroyer at sunset. Secured from G.Q. at 1930. Sea very rough at midnight.

January 6–Clear and hot, but becoming calm. Dawn G.Q. at 0700. Went to G.Q. at 0930 to bombard the shore in Lingayen Gulf. Battle force consisting of 3 battleships, 4 cruisers and destroyers. Started firing at the beach at 1055. We are about 5 miles from the beach. We started numerous fires and set fire to a tanker. At 1130 saw five Jap suicide planes dive. One hit the battleship New Mexico, one hit next to an Australian cruiser and one was hit and exploded over the battleships. At 1200 the destroyers Walke and Sumner of our squadron were hit by suicide planes while operating inshore with the minesweepers. The Sumner's fantail was blown off and the Walke was hit on the bridge killing the Captain and 12 men. Around 1400, I was on deck getting some air when the destroyer O'Brien passed us on our starboard beam. A suicide plane dove over our ship and just missed hitting the O'Brien by 20 feet. A few seconds later one dove on us and all guns fired as it approached and we hit the plane. It exploded on our bow spraying gasoline all over the ship. Parts of the plane and pilot were found all over the ship. Pieces of wiring, a condenser (which was made in the USA), the pilot's fingers, an arm, flesh and clothing were found. About two minutes later another dove on us and was shot down narrowly missing the ship as it crashed into the water. All this took place when we were with the minesweepers about a mile off shore. Later we stopped to pick up a floating body that was blown off the destroyer Sumner. The doctor operated on him all afternoon. He had numerous flesh burns and shrapnel wounds. We fired at floating mines near the ship. Secured from G.Q. at

1930. Battle force retired from the beach. We are supposed to go in again in the morning.

January 7 —Clear, warm and calm. Went to G.Q. at 0230 with contact on surface craft. We fired on it and set it afire off the beach. Went to G.Q. at 0700. We went in about 800 yards off the beach with minesweepers and were off shore all day. Carrier based planes bombed all along the beach setting many fires. The sailor from the Sumner died last night and burial services were held in the afternoon. No enemy planes seen all day until 1900 when one crashed into an LPD.

January 8–Clear, hot and calm. G.Q. at 0700. We went in very close to the beach to resume the minesweeping operation. We still are in Lingayen Gulf and shooting at floating mines. Bombers based on carriers bombed and strafed the beach all day starting fires and blowing up an ammo dump. Battleships and cruisers bombed the beach till dark. Secured from G.Q. at 1930. Tomorrow the invasion is to take place.

January 9–Clear, hot and calm. Battleships and cruisers bombed the beach at 0600. G.Q. at 0630. A Jap plane dropped a bomb between us and a cruiser. We fired at a Jap plane overhead around 0700. The troops started to land at 0645. All types of ships are in the invasion—battleships, cruisers, destroyers, transports, floating dry docks, tankers, LCI's, LST's etc. There are supposed to be 100,000 men landing in this invasion. In the last 3 days the task force has shot down over 100 suicide planes and they have crashed into 17 ships damaging them. The cruiser Columbia was hit and a Rear Admiral was killed on the New Mexico. The ships bombed the beach all day with troops and Higgins boats going in. Around 0600, the New Mexico, our ship and another destroyer went up to the beach to bombard a bridge inland to cut off the Japs retreat. At 1800 a Jap suicide plane dove on our destroyer. A few minutes later one cut across our bow and we fired on it. On the way back to the task force a lone Jap bomber dropped a bomb between us and the New Mexico. We dropped anchor at 2000 off the beach and are supposed to fuel soon.

January 10 —Clear, calm and hot. We fueled the ship at 0235 from the PA ship. Underway at 0700. Fired at a Jap suicide plane, it dove at another ship and then hit the water. During the night the Japs came out in small boats and put time charges on the ships. Two LST's, a PA and a destroyer were damaged. During the day we acted as a fire support group with the Portland, Minnesota, Pennsylvania, Colorado, California, Mississippi, New Mexico and West Virginia. Secured from G.Q. at 1945. Underway all night with the battleships as an outer screen.

January 11–Clear, rough and cool. Now in the South China Sea off Luzon heading north. We went to dawn G.Q. at 0700 and met the carrier force around 0830. We are now with 5 battleships, 2 cruisers and 6 carriers. We met another carrier force around 1600 and now have 12 carriers with us. No dope as to where we are going. We heard over the ships radio that our casualties on the landing were 2 killed 7 injured. The air field was in use 24 hours after the invasion. No enemy planes sighted today.

January 12–Cloudy and rough with high winds and cool. We are still in the South China Sea off Lingayen Gulf with the battle force. Dawn G.Q.a t 0700. G.Q. called at 1000 after radar contact with planes. We were supposed to fuel today, but it was too rough.

Editor's Note–For unexplained reasons, the activity of recording events falls off dramatically after January 12th. After being so diligent for two-and-a-half years, a possible reason may be that Fran's diary could have been discovered by an officer who ordered him, for security reasons, to stop making entries.

January 19, 1945

Dear Folks,

This is my first opportunity to do any writing in quite some time as we have been pretty "busy" lately. I can now tell you that we were in the invasion of Lingayen Gulf on Luzon. This was the third one for us. I'm well and OK and feeling fine thanks to your prayers and offerings Mother.

We haven't received any mail since Jan.1 so I imagine we will have a big bunch when it does get through. I suppose I still have some Christmas packages coming as the only ones I rec'd up until now were the one's you sent Mother and Hartmans. I'm still looking forward to that chocolate cake Ma. Even if it's all crumbs I'll eat it with a spoon. Those cookies you sent were swell Mother and not a one was spoiled. We sat up half the night eating cookies and drinking coffee.

We have been having a couple of hot pinochle games lately. A couple of the fellows and myself get together and play three or four hands. I'll bet I could give Jim Anderson a good game ha! ha!. I just came from a show some of the fellows put on up on the forecastle. It was really good. They have organized a band with drums, a trumpet and guitar. One made a bass fiddle out of a five gallon can, a piece of cord and a long stick. They put on a few acts and were really funny. Well, enough for me.

How is everyone? Fine I hope. According to what we hear it must be pretty cold back home. We heard that you have been having sleet, snow and zero degree weather. Boy! it must be the coldest winter in some time. I suppose Pete and Butz are getting all the sledding and skating they want. Do you have any trouble getting the "green beetle" started in the morning Dad? What's the latest news at home? Have any of the fellows been home on leave lately? I can't wait until some of the Press's come through so I can read some news, even if it is old.

I'll have to bring this to a close now folks. I'll write more later. Until then give my regards to everyone at home. Thinking of you and sending all of my love.

January 20, 1945

Dear Folks,

Just a few more lines to let you know that I'm feeling fine and OK so don't worry. We can now say that we were in the invasion on Lingayen Gulf on Luzon, (censored). I could tell you a lot, but couldn't because of censorship. I have a lot of souvenirs, but can't send them home just yet.

How is everyone? Are you still snow-bound? I'm beginning to forget what snow looks like. I haven't seen it for so long. How are you doing Pete? I suppose by now you have had lots of ice skating. Playing any basketball or doing any dancing? How is school? Chief Triebels still there? I'm going to try and send those shirts and souvenirs for you and Butz when I get the chance.

Hi there Butz! How are you doing? Are you getting enough snow for sledding? I'll bet you and Spot have a good time in it. I'll send you that pennant when I get the chance Butz. How about writing me a few lines when you get time?

Hello Mother. Well I guess you're kinda glad now that the holiday rush is over. I suppose you have the tree all packed away again. I still have some of that Christmas tree hanging over my bunk and it really smells good. Sure miss your cooking and baking Ma. I'll bet I eat you out of house and home when I get back. Have you heard any news from Skin, Al or John lately? I guess I'll have a letter from them when we start getting our mail again. We still haven't received any since the 1st of January. Don't forget what I told you about my monthly check Ma. You take out what you need every month and bank the rest for me.

Hi Dad! How's things going? Sure enjoy your letters. Had a good laugh about your poetry and trick playing. Well I'll have to close for now folks. Give my regards to all as I can't write to everyone. Love to you all.

January 29, 1945

Dear Folks,

Hello everyone, guess what? Our mail arrived today. And Boy! if you want to see a happy looking bunch of fellows you should see us now. It was the first mail we received in a month and did we hit the jackpot. We had thirty bags for us in all. I received 45 letters, 10 newspapers and two more Christmas packages from Mother and Aunt Helen. They ran from way back in October until the latest one which was Jan. 17th. I received Dad's #1 letter and # 1, 2, & 3 from Ma.

I also received several letters from Vince and Butz. Some of the Press's were from way back as far as September. But out here old news was good to read. And I'll probably be reading them over and over again. So now you can see how our mail service runs out here, we don't receive any for some time and then we get it all at once. Up until now Mother I haven't received the chocolate cake, but have received five packages from you. I haven't received Deitrich's, Aunt Clara's or Aunt Jo's. Boy! at this rate I'll be answering letters until the war ends. But it doesn't worry us fellows, the more the better. Oh yes, it took the mail clerk from 7 o'clock until 2 in the morning to sort all this mail.

I'm well and feeling fine folks, but only wish we had some of that snow and sleet you wrote about. Because it is really hot and I do mean hot. Almost everyone has the heat rash from sweating so much and sometimes it itches so it gives you the St. Vitus Dance. But that's where that talcum powder you sent comes in handy Mother. Everything you sent has been useful to me and not a thing broken or smashed. And Ma I'll bet it was due to the metal you put in each package. Because some of the fellows packages were so smashed you couldn't even tell who had sent them. I was glad to hear that all of you had a nice and snowy Christmas and I want to thank all for all you sent me as it made my Christmas a happy one after all. I still have those sprigs of Christmas tree hanging in my bunk and it leaves a nice smell all around. Louise Hartman sent me a sprig of mistletoe, but it doesn't do any of us sailors any good out here ha! ha!

Well Dad I read in your No. 1 letter that you're up to your old tricks again. Boy! did I get a good laugh out of that recipe and joke you pulled about the baby's bottle. You don't know it Dad, but I'm not the only one who has a good laugh out of your practical jokes. I told some of the fellows about your poems and trick playing and now they ask me if I'd heard from you lately and if you're doing any new tricks. (You'd better keep tabs on him Ma with all those girls in his department ha! ha!).

Boy! Mother you certainly made my mouth water when you described that dinner you prepared. Talking about making home made bread and pies and keeping lots of milk on hand for me. I'll bet when I do get home I'll keep Roy Combs working overtime as I haven't tasted any fresh milk for about four months. I went to Mass and received communion on Sunday aboard another ship Ma so you don't have to worry about me on that score as I attend Mass and try and receive whenever I have the opportunity. As you said in your letters Mother maybe your prayers weren't answered for me to be home for Christmas, but they certainly helped me in many other ways. Because we really had some close calls lately with those so and so's.

Hi Vince—well you and Butz really showed me with cards and letters this time. I really want to congratulate you on your swell football playing and getting your letter. I'm proud of you. In one of John Pippen's letters he told me you really accomplished more this year than he did in three years. Glad to hear you're working for Jack again. Even having an assistant too. Boy! maybe you'll be his co-partner pretty soon as you probably bring him lots of customers. Well I finally was able to get the packages wrapped and censored. I'll send them as soon as I can get some stamps from the mail clerk. I hope they will arrive OK as you will probably get the package after you receive this letter. The pocket of the blue shirt is torn a little Pete as I was trying it on to see how I would look in a civilian shirt and I noticed it. But Ma can fix it for you. Boy, wait until Dad gets his grass skirt. I can see him in it now. Ha! Ha.!.

Hello there Butz, sure was glad to hear you received all those swell gifts for Christmas. In one of your letters you said you were wearing long pants. Boy I'll never recognize you when I get home. You say you got some records and a playing phonograph. I'll bet you will be going to dances and jitterbugging like Pete soon. Don't let Pete tease you when the package comes Butz as I have something for each one and a pennant for you. I had a letter from Skin and he also wishes he could meet me. He never can say much, but if we ever meet we would sure have alot to tell each other. I heard from John and he seems to have his wish about getting a ship, but he'll find out for himself. He started signing his letters "landlubber". He sure was glad he got home and saw his brother. I suppose Al Russo and he both will be headed this way. Ray Claus claims he's getting a ship, but I guess the war will end before it's finished. It seems everyone you wrote about is either in France or Germany. But when we all come home from all parts of the world we can really celebrate and say we're glad to be home. Saw Joe Ganke, but not George Nowicki. Joe didn't know me, but I knew him. The last I heard I think he hurt himself some how.

Well folks what do you think of this letter? I'd better close before I exhaust my supply of ink. I'll close hoping to hear from all of you soon, hope you are all well and in good health. Give my regards to everyone and tell them I was asking about them. Thinking of you all and sending my love.

P.S. Enclosed is a little souvenir to add to my collection.

January 31, 1945

Dear Folks,

Well here's a few more lines to let you know I'm well and feeling fine. Boy! after that ten page letter the other night I hardly have anything to write about now. In the past few days I still have received some more letters and I suppose I have received 50 letters in the past two days. I also received another package from Aunt Helen. I'm enjoying the "goodies" I've received from everyone and reading the Press's. I don't believe I ever recall being more glad to receive mail than this time. I only hope I'll be able to write to everyone and thank them and not forget anyone. In the meantime will you tell everyone I've mentioned I received their packages and thank them for me until I can write?

Folks I hope you'll excuse this short letter writing on my part, but I have about 40 more letters to catch up on . In closing I send all my love and am thinking of you all.

P.S. Folks when you receive this letter don't write to me again until you hear from me as I am expecting a change of address soon. Please tell everyone for me. Maybe you won't hear from me for a little while, but don't worry.

February 4, 1945

Dear Mrs. Yearly,

I'm writing this letter at Fran's request. He told me to write you just before he got transferred yesterday. He is heading back to Frisco and from there I don't know where, but I think it will be Philadelphia to go to school. I'm not sure though. Isn't that swell? I sure wish I was him. In one way I hated to see him go as we really had a swell time together.

Well how are you all back in Riverside? I hear that you have been having some real cold weather. I only wish I could be back there enjoying it myself. You have a swell boy and I'll never forget the times we had on our last leave. I'm sorry I didn't meet up with him sooner. I'm not much at writing letters so I think I will sign off now. If you have time I would appreciate hearing from you. Until then I remain,

As ever,

Hank (Ibbitson)

P.S. If he does get home tell him to be sure and go to Burlington and see my folks.

P.S.S. Say hello to the rest of the family for me.

February 15, 1945

Dear Folks,

A few lines to let you know that I'm OK and feeling fine. Getting lots of sunshine and am now starting to get a little tan. It has been some time since I've written you, but this has been my first opportunity to do any writing. Have you heard from Hank yet? He said he was going to write to you. Did you receive the package that I sent about a week or two ago?

I hope this letter finds all of you in good health and are well. I'm wondering how the wintry weather is back home. Are you still having lots of sleet and snow? I guess you're getting a good workout with your sled, huh Butz?

Well Pete are you still holding your position as assistant manager at Jack's? Maybe you can get me a job as helper after the war huh? Hello Mother. I'll bet you're lighting the good ole fire in the kitchen on those cold days huh? I never did receive your chocolate cake Ma, but sure hope you can make it for me in person soon. I wonder if Skin ever got his that his mother sent him. Ma will do you me a favor, when you get this month's allotment check take out some money and get Dad a case of beer for me. I remember his birthday being today, but out here we can't buy any presents or cards so will you get it for me?

Hi! Dad. "Happy Birthday" and hope you have many, many more of them. Ha! Ha! See I didn't forget you as "Cattie" would say—"let's see, that makes you thirty-nine doesn't it"? Ha! Ha! Boy! if those girls in the shop find out it's your birthday you'd better watch out. Drink one of those beers for me Dad, but don't get drunk ha! ha! Have you heard from any of the fellows? John, Skin or Al? I suppose they're all out this way sooner or later. Wonder how John's going to like being on a ship? Where is Marie's husband Jim now? I think I remember you telling me in one of your letters that he was going to sea again.

Glad to hear Joe G. was home on leave. Too bad he didn't see me. I could have hit him with a stone. Almost saw Bud Nowicki the other day. Is Ray Clauss still in Maryland? Had a letter from him a few weeks ago and he said he was getting home every third weekend. Boy! I wonder when he's going to leave the States. Well that's all for awhile folks. Give my regards to everyone. I'll close thinking of you and send all my love.

P.S. Don't write to me until you hear from me as I'll probably have a new address soon so that my mail won't get mixed up as I probably won't receive any for awhile. Please tell everyone for me.

February 20, 1945

Dear Folks,

Hello everybody! A few more lines to let you know that I'm OK am well and feeling fine so don't worry. I've been transferred from my ship and awaiting transportation back to the states. Has Hank written to you yet?

How is everyone at home? Fine I hope. Is the weather still snowy and cold? Sure wish I could be in some of that weather. I've acquired a pretty good tan now and my back is starting to peel. But I'll bet all of you are bundled up in coats and scarfs. Haven't received any mail in several weeks and I suppose I won't until I have a new address and my mail forwarded to me. So I guess there's no use writing because it won't reach me for some time.

I'll have to make this a short letter folks as I have to get it in before the mail closes. So don't worry if you don't hear from me from time to time. I close sending you all my love.

March 1, 1945

Dear Folks,

Just a few lines again to let you know that I'm OK, well and feeling fine. Also to let you know that I'm now on my way back to the states. When I arrive I'll send a telegram and let you know that I'm in.

Sure getting lots of sunshine and a nice sun tan. Wish you folks at home could have some of it. I suppose I'll probably freeze when I hit the climate in the states. How is everyone? In good health I hope. Is the weather still cold? I'll bet you all are sleeping in feather beds and hugging the kitchen stove. Well folks I'll say so long until you hear from me once again. Give my regards to everyone. Love to you all.

P.S.–Don't write until you hear from me.

March 22 –Arrived at Treasure Island, California from the Pacific on the transport Sea Fiddler.

March 22, 1945
Western Union Telegram

Dear Folks. Arrived Frisco today. Am well. Please wire $100 care Western Union 722 Market Street. Will try call you today. Love to all.

March 23-29–Reclassified on Treasure Island.

March 29, 1945
Western Union Telegram

Dear Folks. Good news. Leaving tomorrow afternoon. See you all soon. Love.

March 30–Left Treasure Island for home and a 30 day leave.

March 30-April 2–Left Oakland, California on the freighter Challenger taking four days and four nights.

April 3–I arrived home at 1130.

May 4–Reported to the Philadelphia Navy Yard at 0800.

May 8–V-E Day–Ending of the war in Europe–Germans surrender.

May 9–Left Philadelphia Navy Yard under orders to report to Treasure Island, San Francisco, California.

May 12, 1945
Salt Lake City, Utah

Dear Folks,

It's now 9:45 at night and here I am in my berth in upper #7 writing a few lines about my trip. We left 24th & Chestnut St. Station in Philadelphia at 2:22. We had our own dinner and Pullman. I'm in a car with about ten other sailors all going to Frisco so we're having a good time of it.

We arrived in Chicago on the second day and had a couple hours lay-over and a chance to look around. At Chicago it was raining and pretty cold too. After that we hit Omaha, Nebraska and it also was rather cold and we had some snow.

After leaving Omaha we took the Rio Grande route which took us through the Rocky Mountains in Colorado. This was some of the most beautiful country I've ever seen. Some of the mountains were so steep we have to have two engines to pull us. I'd sure like to travel through here sometime in a car and enjoy the scenery. It was really beautiful with the snow capped mountains and pine trees, cold trout streams from the mountains winding all along the tracks and herds of cattle and horses. Every once in awhile we would see a mining camp. This snappy mountain air really peps you up.

We hit Denver, Colorado yesterday afternoon and Salt Lake City early today. We spent all this afternoon going through the salt flats and it is really interesting to see how salt water is evaporated and collected. We now are traveling through Nevada with its high mountains and sage brush. Tomorrow we are supposed to hit Frisco around two or three o'clock. We also have pretty good dinner service. Tonight we had turkey.

Well I guess that's all for now folks. I'll write more when I get settled in Frisco. I wish you a "Happy Mother's Day" Mother and a big kiss and hope you get my flowers and card OK. I only wish I could spend it with you. I'll close for now.

P.S. Please excuse this horrible scrawl as I'm propped up in my berth here trying to write while this train is going around curves and jumping up and down about sixty miles so far.

May 13–Arrived Treasure Island, San Francisco, California.

May 14-30–Stayed in receiving ship, Barracks E.

May 15, 1945
San Francisco, Calif.

Dear Folks,

Well here I am writing from "sunny California." again. (Boy!) this Chamber of Commerce should be shot. Believe it or not it has been raining for two days and it's so cold here the fellows are wearing their peacoats. Can you picture that in mid-May in Calif? But I'll bet it's nice in Jersey now because it was a swell day when we left Phila. We traveled over four different railroads, the B&O, Burlington, Rio Grande and Western and the Western Pacific.

So you can see we had a swell chance to see alot of scenery. One can hardly begin to describe the mountains, snow-capped peaks, canyons, mountain streams and desert which we saw coming through Colorado, Utah and Nevada. It was really beautiful. When we left Phila. our Pullman car was on a civilian train until we hit Chicago. Then we attached to a train full of sailors. When we hit Frisco at 5:30 Sunday night we were 12 hours late, but I got a late train statement from the S.P.'s at the station. This later proved useful because my orders read to report in at 8:30 Sunday morning and I almost wound up in the brig for being late, until I showed them my late train statement. So then I was excused. There were a swell bunch of fellows on the train with me and we had a swell time coming across country.

Just now I'm assigned to a temporary barracks until I get moved into the school barracks. I still see a couple of fellows around here that I reported in with. Boy! there must be a million sailors on this base. You can really notice the increase since I was here in March. I went in town on Sunday night, had supper and went to a good show. I saw Wallace Beery in "This Man's Navy". You don't want to miss that when it comes to Riverside. Here on the base last night I saw "The Enchanted Cottage" which was good also. They have alot of entertainment and recreation here, three gymnasiums, three movies, baseball fields, swimming pools and boxing and wrestling shows.

Well how is everything back home? How are your chicks getting along Mother? Did you lose any more? It won't be long before you have some fryers running around. I suppose Pete and Butz are anxiously awaiting the closing of school and summer vacation. Are you still helping Mother with the chicks Butz? I've got a few more pennants for you and I'll send them when I get a chance. It won't be long before you'll be going to Prom huh Pete? Have you seen any new fellows home on leave? If you get a chance will you put some new sand in the pigeon coop and throw in some tobacco stems? Don't let them raise any more squabs after this month though.

Say Dad did you get to play any more jokes in the factory? Who was in that bout down at Camden on Monday night, Evans or Martinelli? We'll have to see a few more good bouts when I get home again. Dad I'm sending home those two certificates that I got when I was on the Simpson. Will you put them away somewhere for me?

Mother would you send me some literature from home? I forgot to bring it with me when I left. It's in the right hand side of the bookcase and from the Philadelphia College of Pharmacy and Science. There are a few booklets or pamphlets that they sent to me when I graduated from high school. I have a few more with me from some of the other colleges and I want to read up on them and get an idea what I want to study after the war. I'll have to close for now as it's time to go over to chow. Give my regards to everyone at home.

P.S. Mother if any mail comes for me at the house will you please forward it to me?

May 19, 1945
San Francisco

Dear Folks,

Hello everyone how is everything at home? Has it started to get real warm yet? Well this "balmy" weather has finally cleared up for awhile. This is the second nice day we've had in a row. But at night it gets pretty breezy.

I'm now in the Pre-Commissioning barracks and so my address changes again. It's Building 151 instead of 173. I haven't received any mail as yet and I suppose I won't for awhile. Between my mail in Philadelphia and Bldg. 173 it will be awhile before they locate me.

The setup seems to be about the same as it was in Norfolk. We are to attend combat swimming, fire fighting school and instructions in gas drill. Then we get sent to a school for our rate. In that case mine would be in boilers, which is a four week course in itself. I was talking to one fellow and he says he was here four months before he was assigned to a ship. Boy! the longer the better because this doesn't seem to be a bad place and there's always something to do. With three theaters, two ball diamonds, two ship service stores, two bowling alleys, two gymnasiums, two swimming pools and a pistol range there's always plenty of opportunity for relaxation.

I saw a good picture at theater #3 the other night called "The Affairs of Susan". Boy! that was a riot and funny too. On Wednesday afternoon we went down to the pistol range and fired a few rounds of target practice. Tuesday morning a few fellows and I bowled a few games, but darn it I couldn't break over 112. Yesterday afternoon we went down to the gym and played a little basketball. That place has everything, a boxing ring, badmitton courts, tumbling mats, weight lifting apparatus and punching bags.

Well I'm finally in a place that my rate and sea experience means something. The other morning I was detailed to drill and march sixteen men.

Boy! you should have heard me with colors right!! colors left!! and double to the rear. I really had them going. We rated men here also get out of the work details too which are given to the non-rated men or seamen.

Last night I went to a dance at the University of California, whic is in Berkley, about fifteen miles from here. It was given by one of the girl's sororities for the sailors. There were about twenty of us fellows and we had a swell time. The dance was held in a big rustic building which had a big stove fireplace. Believe it or not we even had a little fire going because it was rather chilly. They had refreshments for us and we all enjoyed ourselves. How is everything in Riverside? Are there any new fellows home on leave? How are the young chicks doing Mother? Are they growing very much?

Well folks, I'll have to make this letter rather short as the lights are just about ready to go out. Give my regards to everyone at home.

P.S.–Don't forget to use the new address.

Postcard
May 23, 1945
San Francisco, Calif.

Dear Folks,
    Sure feels great to be back in the states again. This is a swell place and the people are very nice. Am now in the city on 48 hr pass and enjoying the sights. Hope to see you all soon.

May 25, 1945
San Francisco, Calif.

Dear Folks,

Hello everyone! How is everything in Riverside? Fine I hope. Has the weather become very warm yet? Don't let anyone fool you about "basking in the California sunshine" take it from me. Here it is almost June and the other night I slept with two blankets on. It stays fairly warm up until two in the afternoon and then the wind kicks up and it really gets chilly. I still wear my peacoat when I go out at night.

Guess what? The other day I bumped into a fellow from Riverside here. His name is Matthew Murray and he's also attached to the Pre-Commission school. I graduated in "42" with his sister Dot Murray. He looks an awful lot like Skin. Maybe Pete knows him. We see each other almost every day at noon. In fact he's in the same barrack as me, but just across the way. I've also bumped into alot of fellows here who came back from the Islands with me on the ole "Sea Fiddler".

I saw some pretty good shows on the base this past week. Last night the Shell Show was at Theatre #3. This was sponsored by Shell Oil Co. and included a dancer, ventriloquist, singer, magician and comedian who could really play a tricky harmonica. It was a swell show and the fellows got alot of laughs from it.

Well Mother yesterday I received my first mail. It was two letters from you and dated around the 15th. They first went to the directory service before they located me. Today I received one from Doris in Germantown so I guess it will be catching up to me gradually. Thanks for forwarding Skin's letter. He was glad to hear from me and he talked as if he expects to be out there for some time yet.

Mother will you send me a few Press's occasionally so I can keep up on the news? How are your chicks doing? Did you lose any more? Hi Butz did you receive your pennant yet? How did you like the one from Alcatraz? Hello Pete, how's the clerk coming along? Have they held the

Prom yet? Who are you taking? (the lucky girl). Hi! Dad—How are you doing? How is your garden coming along? Have you been down to any more bouts? I see by the paper you'll be getting more gas now (better watch your coupons Ha! Ha!).

I'm enclosing a clipping from tonight's paper. This is the Destroyer Laffery, sister ship to the Barton who was with us at Normandy and the Philippines. She got hit like that at Okinawa and probably was with Hank. If there are any pictures in the Jersey paper will you clip it and save it for me? Well I'll sign off for now folks and hope to be hearing from you soon. Give my regards to everyone at home.

June 1–July 1–Stayed at the destroyer pool for further assignment to a new construction destroyer.

June 4, 1945
San Francisco, Calif.

Dear Folks,

Hello everyone, how's everything back in Riverside? Fine I hope. I just can picture the swell weather you must be having this month. This Frisco weather is certainly a puzzle, one day its like Spring and the next it's windy or rainy. Well it looks as if my mail is finally straightened out as it is beginning to arrive fairly regular now. Mother I've received all the letters you forwarded, the literature you sent and your last letter of May 31st which I received on June 2nd. But occasionally I received some mail which went out to the ship and was sent back here. The other day I received a letter from Bernie dated Jan. 6th and today received one from you dated Feb. 5. That one seemed rather funny as you were describing the zero weather you were having there. I just received a portrait picture from Carolyn also which was sent on Feb. 5th, went out to ship and finally arrived here after traveling for four months. This was the same case as Aunt Elise's package as I suppose I was one jump ahead of it whenever I moved.

Well folks I've got some good news. Al & I met out here and went out together on Friday. When I received your letter saying he hit Calif. I was glad, but you didn't say if he was in San Diego or Frisco. So I wrote him a letter right away thinking if his ship was in Frisco he would receive it and look me up. The following day I happened to be walking down near the waterfront and looking out in the bay I saw Al's ship, a big 62 painted on her come steaming in. The next day I had just entered the barracks in the afternoon when they passed the word over the P.A. system that I had a visitor. Sure enough, there was Al.

It was fortunate I had liberty the same night so we could go out together. He had one of his buddies from the ship with him and we went out and had some pictures taken and spent a swell evening together. Yesterday I was supposed to meet him at the Pepsi Cola Center in Frisco around one o'clock, but I waited two hours and he didn't show up. He told me they expected to leave soon, but he thought they would be back in about six weeks. He looked good and has a tan just like I had when I came back. He said that they were in the invasion of Okinawa and he saw the Barton there just before he left.

Speaking of the ole Barton I haven't had a letter from Hank since I was home. However, I did receive a letter from my other buddy, Bob Glatz who is from Haddon Heights. He said that since I left the "Ole Busy B" has had her "box score" repainted up on the bridge. A Nazi plane and several pill boxes representing the invasion of Normandy and seven Jap planes and two surface ships, also six hash marks representing six invasions. Some record, huh? There has been quite alot of entertainment on the base this past week, two USO shows and an indoor circus. In fact I think it was the same one which Dad and Butz saw in Burlington. Polack Bros. Circus, that was it, wasn't it?

On Saturday night the Hollywood Review from Hollywood played here. It featured Groucho Marx as Master of Ceremonies and several of the smaller stars including dancers, magicians, singers and comedians. That Groucho Marx is funnier in person than he is on the screen. He had the fellows in "stitches" all the time. Well even the Navy has been hit by rationing. Starting on Friday, and in all the 48 states, cigarettes are being rationed. We were issued a ration card and now every time we go to the ship's service store it has to be punched when buying cigarettes or tobacco. Formally we were allowed two packages per day, but now it's only six packages per week. That still won't bother me as I don't smoke as much now as I used to.

Yesterday when I went into Frisco and Al didn't show up I decided to do a little sightseeing as the day was pretty nice. I took a walk out to see the Civic Opera House where the Peace Conference is being held. It really is a beautiful and colorful building. The street that approaches it is lined on both sides with the flags of all the nations represented. They have lots of MP's and police patrolling around the building and you can't approach near it without showing credentials for the conference,. At night it is illuminated with numerous search lights and really looks pretty, just like the Capitol dome in Washington. While I was walking around there one of the foreign delegates passed me, he had a long black beard and looked very dignified.

They have wrestling bouts in Frisco at the Civic Auditorium on Tuesday nights so tomorrow night I think I will go see them. Have you been down to Camden since I left Dad? I guess that mauler Evans is still winning huh? Treasure Island has a baseball team here so I've seen a few ball games. A few of the fellows and I went down to the gym the other day and played a little basketball. I weighed myself and by the scales I picked up four pounds so now I weigh 164. We had some good chicken yesterday for Sunday chow, but not as good as you make Mother.

How are your chicks doing Mother? I wouldn't be too afraid of putting those two sick ones back in with the others if they look OK now.

The most dangerous time for cocci is from 4-6 weeks. But if the litter is kept dry it won't break out. Say Pete, when are you going to break down and write me a letter about the Prom? Mother said you looked pretty sporty that night. How were your exams, very hard? Hi Butz!, did you receive the pennants I sent? I hear you've been working pretty hard white washing trees. Are you going to work at Banyas this summer? Hello Dad, how's your garden coming along? The "jet-propelled" green bettle still holding up? I suppose you're getting more gas now huh? I saw the first "45" Ford in the paper the other day. Guess they'll start production again now. Well when I get out we'll really get a good one, then you and Ma can relax in the back seat and let Vince and I do all the driving. I guess it won't be long before Butz is putting the car in the garage.

Well folks I have to close for now as the lights are about to go out. Hope to hear from you soon. Give my regards to everyone at home.

June 11, 1945
San Francisco, Calif.
8:30 PM

Dear Folks,

This morning I received your letter of June 6th and special delivery letter of June 8th. Mother I'm sorry I had you worried about me not writing and wondering if I was sick or something. I missed doing any writing last week because several nights I went out to see the USO shows on the base and had the weekend off. So you see it wasn't a case of me not wanting to write or anything like that. I suppose I was so occupied I just let it slip by. Then too I've been addressing all my States Mail Free so I guess that's why it is taking you longer to receive it. I will send this letter air mail so let me know how soon it reaches you.

I've been fine and "in the pink". I'm getting lots of sunshine and exercise now and eating alot. Out here we get lots of tomatoes, lettuce and salads, which I crave. I've been weighing myself on a regular basis and gaining slowly, but surely. I think I've gained 7 pounds since I've been here. The school setup is that you don't start attending until you're attached to a ship's detail. Until then we Petty Officers are getting a good break. During the day we go with the physical instructor and can either play baseball, basketball, go swimming in the pool, bowling, use the recreation center, library, pistol range or do anything we want in regard to recreation and exercise. We get every other night liberty and every third weekend.

The Murray boy from Riverside was here three weeks before he was assigned and is just now starting his school. His ship doesn't even go into commission until August. I'll be here a month on Wednesday and so far no signs of being assigned yet. I'm not complaining as we fellows have a swell time during the day with the above activities. I talked to one fellow the other day who has been here 5 ½ months. So who knows, maybe I'll be here until September. I sure hope so because this staying on solid "terra firma" for awhile really feels good. Ha! Ha!

The weather over the weekend and past few days has been exceptionally beautiful. Even the weatherman said so in tonight's paper. The temperature yesterday was 77 degrees and nice, warm and sunny. I guess you will receive that record I made at the Pepsi-Cola Center in a few days. What do you think of it? I guess Butz will get a big kick out of playing it. As I told you on the record, myself and some of the fellows spent a swell weekend sightseeing. The Golden Gate Park here in Frisco is beautiful. Yesterday was so nice and everyone was out there enjoying themselves sunbathing and rowing on the lake. The Aquarium, Museum of Natural History and art galleries are also located here, which we visited. We saw all sorts of exhibits from the 14th century until the present day.

On Saturday night we slept and stayed at the Navy Mothers Club. They were really swell to us and made us feel right at home. All of them had sons in the service. At six o'clock they served us a big supper and that night had a dance with hostesses and entertainment. Around midnight we had coffee and cake. That night we slept in a swell bunk and they let us sleep until 10:30 Sunday morning. When we awoke they had a big breakfast for us. Then I went to twelve o'clock Mass at St. Peters which is just about two blocks from the club.

I had a letter from John with his usual short remarks. Have you heard from him lately? Boy! I was surprised in reading your letter about Bernie being engaged. Those Florida southern belles are really hooking em. First Emil and now Bernie. Wait till I drop him a line–haven't heard from Skin in a few weeks. Had a letter from George Banyas talking about his leave. Also I wrote and heard from that fellow in Virginia whose letter you forwarded to me. He's going to school there, but I'd much rather be in Calif. than that place.

I received Vince's letter on Friday, but so far no Press's. I guess they'll arrive eventually though. Boy Vince, after hearing of Snyder and your adventures in the big city I came to the conclusion that you two desperados would do most anything. Ha! Ha! So Ray Clauss has finally put to sea, huh? Will you send me his address so I can drop him a line? Has "Letch" or Larry Yearly started home yet? Have you heard from Bill or Ernie?

How are the chicks doing Ma? They should be pretty big by now. Has Uncle Carl vaccinated them yet? Mother told me you fixed my pigeon coop up Dad, thanks alot. Tell Butz he can give them a bath every once in awhile. What are you going to do with the summer Butz? Get a job working for Banyas? How's your cub pack doing? Say Pete you didn't say anything in your letter about this Merchant Marine. What do you mean just for the summer? Boy! if you don't go back to school and graduate next fall you're going to hear from your big brother when I get home again. I mean it.

Well folks I hope this letter makes up for me not writing last week as I will try to write more often. It's almost time for "lights out so I'll close sending my love to you all.

San Francisco, Calif.
June 12, 1945

Dear Mother,

I received your letter yesterday in which you said that Vince is think-ing about the Merchant Marine. I wasn't too surprised as I thought as soon as I left he would be getting restless and try something else.

Just what does he mean by joining just for the summer? Is this just a training program ashore or do they actually go to sea? If it's just for the summer and ashore I think it would do him alot of good. But Mother I'm afraid if he does go in he won't want to go back to school in the fall and graduate.

If you and Dad do decide to let him go in I would make it plain to him and only under one provision that he finishes school first. Don't let him talk you out of it. After he finishes school and graduates then it will be up to him what he wants to do. Now Mother don't let him influence you as to what to do as that's up to you and Dad. But as you asked my opinion I thought I would tell you what I thought.

It's another swell day with a clear sky overhead and nice and warm. If fact its getting a little warm for blues now. We have a swell library on the base. On my duty nights I've been reading up on chemistry. I sent to the Philadelphia College of Pharmacy and Science for more literature and particulars. If I have the opportunity when the war is over I'd like to take it up again.

I've become acquainted with a new bunch of fellows in the barracks and we've been having a good time. One is from North Carolina and the other from Oklahoma. The other night I met a bunch of fellows from New Jersey, New Brunswick and the Oranges. That's one good thing about the service, you meet alot of fellows from all over. I'll close for now Mother as I have a little more writing to do before the one o'clock muster. Give my regards to everyone at home.

P.S. If you see any of the Hartman girls tell them to write as I haven't heard from them yet, although I've written to them.

June 18, 1945
San Francisco, Calif.

Dear Folks,

Here it is another beautiful day with the sun shining brightly and a blue sky over head. It has been like this for a week now with the temperature in the high 80's. We can start appreciating this California sunshine. I talked to a fellow who has lived here five years and he said this has been exceptionally nice weather for this time of the year.

Well I guess I can't complain about not receiving any mail as I've really been flooded with it in the past few days. I received all your Press's Thursday of last week Mother. Thanks alot. On Friday I received letters from Butz, Aunt Helen, Skin, John and Hank. Today I received your letter of the 14th and one from Aunt Elise. So now I'll really have some writing to do.

The letter from Skin took ten days to get here. He said he saw the Barton in the last port he was in. I imagine he may either be in Saipan or Guam by now as Hank said in his letter that they were there recently. He also said that they may have added a submarine to the Barton's box score, but didn't know for sure. Had a letter from Al which took six days so I guess he's back out in the islands again.

I had this past weekend off again so another fellow and I were off to see the sights. After Captain's Inspection on Saturday we went out to the Navy Mothers Club where we had a big supper. Afterward we went into town to see the Ice Follies. We had $3 seats right next to the ice. It was really a swell and colorful show and I enjoyed it alot.

After the show we went back to the club where they had coffee and cake for us and hostesses who came in to dance. We slept until 10:30 on

Sunday and then we got up and had a breakfast of cereal, bacon and eggs. I went to 11:00 Mass which was a Pontifical High Mass. On Sunday afternoon we took a trolley and went to the beach. It was swell with a nice cool ocean breeze blowing. There must have been a couple thousand people. We also saw the famous seal rocks which are covered with seals and are just a little off shore. We ate dinner at the internationally famous Cliff House which is a big restaurant on the edge of a high cliff overlooking Frisco bay. From here while you are eating you can see miles out to sea and all along the beach with the city in the background. After that we went up to the Heights which is even up higher yet. From there you can see everything for miles. So we had a busy weekend and swell time. We could never make it to Los Angeles or Hollywood from here, which is 495 miles. But there are still plenty of places to see and go to here in Frisco.

How is everyone at home? I imagine the weather is pretty stifling by now. I'm glad your chicks are doing so well Mother. They should really be growing fast in that nice weather. Hello Dad did you have a good time at the doggie roast? Did you receive my card? I sent you the money so you could get what you want as I couldn't find anything out here to send that you would like to have. Hi Butz, I received your nice long letter on Friday. Thanks alot. I'll bet you're glad now that school's over huh? Did the record come yet?

Hi Pete, what's new in Riverside? Has school closed yet? How's the swimming up at the lakes this year? I hope you've given up joining the Merchant Marines by now. Well folks I must bring this to a close as I have alot of writing to do. Give my regards to everyone at Home. Love to all.

P.S. Mother will you send me Ray Clauss's address in your next letter?

June 26, 1945
San Francisco, Calif.

Dear Folks,

Well after one whole week of beautiful warm weather we are now wearing peacoats again, believe it or not. Last Sunday was the warmest with a recorded temperature of 95. On Monday a fog rolled in from the bay and it cooled things off.

I received Dad's letter on Friday and one from Mother yesterday. Also received a fruit cake from the Barton you sent Mother and a Press of Oct. 26, 1944. Boy! they must have circled the globe. The fruitcake was intact and still fresh. A few of my buddies and I had it one night before we went to bed.

I haven't written this week as I have been waiting to accumulate some news. By now I have lots to write. On Sunday one of my buddies and I met at the Golden Gate Theatre, one of the biggest in Frisco. Right in the middle of the stage show who walks up and taps me on the shoulder but Al Russo. Boy! was I surprised. Here he was sitting in the same row as we were and spotted me first. He said they had just come in from Pearl Harbor that morning and he called up my barracks and found out I wasn't there so he and his buddy decided to go to a show. Of all the places to meet here in Frisco it had to be in a crowded movie. Talk about coincidences.

So the four of us went out and had a good time together. We had dinner and went over to Oakland and went roller skating. We then shot some pool and went bowling. Al said they expect to be in about two weeks so we should see alot of each other. It's really fortunate that we're both in the same place so it's just like being home together again.

On Saturday night we went out to the Mothers Club and they had a show and dance afterward. I believe I'm seeing more stage shows on the base than if I'd have been in Hollywood. There's an average of two or three Hollywood and USO shows a week. Last Friday Linda Darnell was here in person. Last night Kay Kaiser, his band and radio show were here. He was really good and kept the fellows in stitches for about two hours. Eddie Bracken and Peggy Ryan are appearing in person at theatre #3 tonight so I guess I'll see that show too.

Last night they brought a Jap eleven man cargo submarine in and had it open for inspection for a few days. It was sunk, refloated and captured at Lingayen Gulf in the Philippines. I went aboard and all through it. You would be surprised at how many things were made in the USA and lots of things plainly marked Tokyo. I "hooked" a porcelain light socket from the radio panel in the radio room and sure enough it was made in the USA. The inside of the sub was all corroded from being under water and just smelled of Japs.

Well folks I guess you have been reading about the big time going on here in Frisco this week. On Monday I saw my first President. I put in for early liberty at two o'clock and went and saw the parade. He arrived at the field at 2:30 in Oakland and then came to Frisco via the Golden Gate Bridge. The parade came down Market St., which is Main St. in Frisco, about four o'clock. I had a good view right by the curb so I had a good look at him. The head of the parade was led by a motorcycle escort then came President Truman in an open car standing and waving. In the following cars were representatives of each country at the conference. You should have seen those from Saudia Arabia with their robes and headdress. In all the parade contained 75 cars. I never saw so many people in all my life, they were standing on street cars, office buildings, corners and everywhere. When the President passed everyone cheered and applauded and a shower of paper floated down from the tops of the office buildings.

How's everyone at home? I suppose it's good swimming weather now, isn't it? I hope all of you have a swell time on your vacation next week. Take it easy and enjoy yourselves. Give my regards to everyone up North Jersey way and tell them I was asking about them. Did you receive that book I sent about Treasure Island yet? Say Butz, I think you'll be receiving something by mail this week. Write and tell me how you like it. Well folks I had better close now so you will receive this letter. Because you're probably wondering what happened to me ha! ha!. Love to you all.

June 28, 1945
San Francisco, Calif.

Dear Folks,

Enclosed is a booklet of views of San Francisco I thought you would like to see. Some of the places I have already visited are the "Cliff House" which is pictured opposite that of Alcatraz, San Francisco's Ocean Beach and Amusement Park where the conference was held, and University of California campus and Golden Gate Park.

The clipping of the Nashville is of Joe G.'s ship which was with us when she was hit. The green clipping was photographed at the Navy Mothers Club last Saturday night when they had a show for us. Do you recognize that sailor in the background by the piano? Yep, it's me. Boy! was I surprised when I saw it in today's paper. A newspaper photographer was there taking different pictures of the club. You should have seen one he took of myself, another sailor and a marine drying dishes in the kitchen .That was best of all, but I guess they didn't want to give the impression that you had to wash dishes when you went there ha! ha!.

I'm also sending a copy of T.I.'s paper, The Masthead. The picture of the pistol tournament on page 8 is the one I was in. Believe it or not I'm in that picture somewhere, but you would probably need a microscope to find me I'm back so far. Let me know if you receive all these clippings and paper will you? So long for now.

July 2–Assigned to the USS Buck and transferred to barracks C.

July 2, 1945
San Francisco, Calif.

Dear Folks,

Hello everyone. I received your letter of the 26th on Friday and was very glad to hear from you. I'm glad you had such a swell time at Irvington last week. Boy! that must have been a riot with Jim, John and Dad together. I hope you have as nice a time up to Penn Argyle this week.

The weather has been rather chilly the past few days with the temperature in the low 60's. I saw in the paper that the temp. in Washington was 90 so I suppose it was pretty hot in Jersey also. Are you doing much swimming now Pete & Butz? Don't forget and drop me a line again when you have time.

What are you doing with yourself now that school is over Butz? I guess you're spending most of your time with the Cubs and at Banyas huh? Say Butz, did that_____I sent you arrive yet? I'll bet you'll never guess what it is. Are you still working at the Paramount Pete? How's the lakes for swimming this year? Have you seen any of the A's games yet? By the looks of their playing in the paper they seem to be lousy as usual. I see most of T.I.'s games and they're pretty good. They have alot of former big league players with them, such as Dick Bartell and Barney Olsen of the New York Giants.

I haven't received your other two Press's or Reviews as yet Mother, but I guess they'll arrive any day now. Did you receive those clippings and book of scenic views I sent? Mother will you send me my basketball shoes? I believe they are up in the cedar chest. We have a wonderful gym and I've been doing quite a bit of exercising and playing basketball.

Hi Dad! how are you enjoying your vacation? I'll bet it feels good to relax and take it easy for awhile huh? How's your garden coming along? Have you picked anything yet? I'm getting a pretty nice tan again eating lots and getting alot of exercise. This week they brought about a thousand German prisoners here. Today I saw them all over working at different places. Some were shoveling dirt, making grass and they even work in the mess hall washing trays.

They wear blue dungarees with a big white PW all over them. They are a pretty healthy looking lot though. Well I guess that's all for now as I have a few more letters to write. Hoping to hear from you soon. Love to all.

P.S. Had a letter from Skin and he said where he's at now is better than the Solomons. He goes ashore to a native village every four days and is allowed two cans of beer. Also had a letter from Bernie and the way he talks he's engaged, but he didn't say anything about giving her a ring!

July 3-18—Went to boiler school on Treasure Island.

July 9, 1945
San Francisco, Calif.

Dear Folks,

I received your letter from Bayonne on Saturday and was very glad to hear from you and that you're having such a good time on your vacation up North Jersey. Was the weather nice all the while you were there? How was your trip to Penn Argyle? Oh, yes Mother, I also received those other Press's and Reviews you sent. It was sure swell to read all the hometown news again.

This past week I started school and so far have been to first aid lectures, chemical warfare school and had a swimming test. In the chemical warfare school we saw movies and got a sniff of the different war gases with, and without, a gas mask. Boy! you should have seen the tear gas make me cry. Ha! Ha! In the swimming test we had to swim the usual 50 yards, jump off a ten-foot turn, then swim to a cargo net, climb up and jump off a twenty-two foot platform into the water. This was the fourth time I took it. Norfolk, Boston, Phila. and now here. They have some swell indoor pools and I was just swimming last week. Every day we go over to the gym and exercise with weights, rowing machines, and punching bags, etc.

Last Wednesday night another fellow and I went in town to the Civic Auditorium and saw the wrestling bouts. We had ringside seats and what a show! The main bout was "Chief" Cherwacki and George Konerley. Konerly won the second fare on a default as the "Chief" produced a wire noose from his thumbs and proceeded to strangle his opponent. Cherwacki is the same fellow who wrestled down in Camden a couple of years ago and pulled a pepper shaker out of his thumbs and put pepper in his opponents eyes when he had him on the mat. In all it was a good show, but nothing like watching those in Camden Dad.

On Sunday I saw Tony Pastor and his Orchestra's stage show at the Golden Gate. Also saw some good shows lately–"Medal for Benny", "Those Endearing Young Charms", "Music for Millions" and "The Great John L.". I haven't heard from Skin or John for a couple of weeks. Had a letter from George Banyas today, he's still down in Texas. Has Ray Claus been home lately? Are "Les" Yearly and Lawrence Yearly still in Europe?

Say Butz, did you receive your_____yet? You should have received it by now. What's new in Riverside Pete, still working at the drug store? How about you two dropping me a line when you have the time huh? Well folks I'll close for now until I have some more news. Hoping to hear from you again soon Give my regards to everyone at home. Love to all.

July 13, 1945
San Francisco, Calif.

Dear Folks,

Received your letter on July 10th and was very glad to hear from you and that you had such a swell trip up to Penn Argyle. I still remember when we used to go up there some time ago even though I was pretty small then. How is the weather in Riverside? Here it has been sunny, but cool toward night. We are still wearing blues. In the northern part of California they wear them all year around because it never gets that hot up in Frisco. It was funny because in San Diego, just 450 miles south of here, they wear whites all year round.

Well folks after being here just two months I've finally been assigned to a new ship. It's the USS Buck (DD761) and just like the Barton. The ship is due to go in commission on September 6 so it still looks like I'll be here all summer and then some. Our crew, except the captain, organized this week and all 320 of us are together in one barracks. It looks like we are going to have a good crew as it is composed of alot of fellows that I've been traveling around with since I came back from leave.

The ship is being built in Frisco so even after we are aboard ship we will still be in here. Our executive officer, who seems to be a pretty swell guy, talked to us yesterday and said the ship was originally due to go into commission last March and has been set back to September for commissioning and still may be set back further yet, according to the way the work is completed. After commissioning we are supposed to get a two weeks fitting out period in the yard and then go on a shakedown cruise for 5-6 weeks. After that it's back in the yard for two more weeks.

So in all I may be around well up until Christmas. Who knows, the war may be over by then. Boy! by the looks of the paper and the pounding they gave Japan this past week it may be over by then. I suppose the ole Barton has been in the middle of it as I haven't heard from Hank in about three weeks. Had a letter from Skin and he said he saw the Barton again in his present port. I think he's in either Okinawa or Guam. Haven't heard from John in a month. I saw a swell USO show and picture last night. Abbott and Costello are playing in a picture called "The Gay Nineties" and it's really good. This afternoon all of my buddies and I went over to the swimming pool and then to the sun deck and absorbed a little of this California sunshine. We then got a steam bath which really pepped us up. Last week I went to the dentist and had a couple of teeth pulled so now they will be okay for another six months ha! ha! Remember Mother when you had to drive me down to Dr. White's to get them fixed?

The reason I sent for the money Mother was since I've not been getting my 20% for sea pay I only draw $11 every two weeks now. As I sent all my clothes to the laundry and my blues to the tailors and with all the liberty and sightseeing I've been doing, well it kinda left me a little short. But Mother make sure you draw it from my account when you send it. Are you taking some out for yourself every month like I told you to? Even if you would just take $10 or so I know it would help you alot. Well folks I must close for now as I have to shine my shoes and prepare for Captain's inspection tomorrow. Give my regards to everyone at home and write soon again. Love to you all.

P.S. Please use my new address.

July 19–The whole crew of the Buck was reassigned to the USS Anderson.

July 19, 1945
San Francisco, Calif.

Dear Folks,

Received three letters from you in the past few days. Pete's letter arrived on Friday, one on Tuesday and Mother I received your long letter today. Also rec'd two Tribunes, but as yet my shoes haven't arrived. Thanks alot for sending the money Mother. I went in town and picked it up last night (Wednesday). Be sure to draw it from my bank account in case you had to use your own money.

I guess you received my previous letter by now telling of my new change of address. On Monday I started Boiler school and will be going to it for a few weeks. Yesterday I was talking to the Chief Water Tender who teaches and was telling him that I was on a "four-piper" for a year. He asked me the name of it and when I said the Simpson he said "why I was on her in China back in 1935". Some coincidence huh? He's a swell chief and has been all around the world. The other day he was telling us about Tokyo when he was over there during peace time.

Speaking of Tokyo what do you think of the headlines this past week? Boy! with all that bombing and bombarding by the fleet it looks like the end is in sight pretty soon. It looks like we're going to have a pretty good crew on the Buck as we have a good bunch of fellows and every day we're meeting someone new. Most of the Petty Officers already have been to sea except some of the firemen and seamen. Today I was talking to one of the fellows who goes down to the ship every day and he said it will be a miracle if it is even completed by September. It is only half-finished and there are only five electricians wiring the whole ship. This week they had a strike in the shipyards and work was stopped altogether for a few days.

On Tuesday I had to go over to the dispensary to get my annual tetanus "shot". I had a sore arm up until yesterday. By now I'm used to them. Last Saturday I saw Tony Pastor's Orchestra at the Golden Gate. Last night I saw Jan Savitt's Orchestra and the picture "Back to Bataan". This was a swell picture, try to see it when it comes to Riverside. I went out to a dance at the Navy Mothers Club on Sunday and had a swell time.

Mother you asked me about getting towels, shorts and sheets. I can get you the towels and shorts, but not sheets. They only have mattress covers and are about the size for the mattress I have at home. Large white turkish towels are 50 cents and the undershirts and shorts are 35 cents. Just write and let me know what you want and the size shorts for Dad, Pete or Butz and I will get them for you.

Had a letter from Skin and he hints pretty strongly that he's at Leyte P.I. At the end of his letter he put a P.S. and asked about the first invasion I was in. So now I'm pretty sure that's where he's at. Also had a letter from Hank and he said they got a new captain, executive officer and chief engineer. He said some of the enlisted men have been transferred since I left. Thanks for your letter Pete. Boy! you must have done O.K. in school with those marks. Tell "Jeep" Cameron I was asking about him. Are there any other fellows around town?

Hi! Butz! Did you receive the turtle yet? Boy! they must have put a tag on his leg addressed it to Riverside and let him swim across country. Are you working back at Banyas? How's the Green Beetle?

Hello Dad–Mother tells me your garden's coming along OK now. With all that rain you had last Sunday everything should be shooting up. How are the pigeons doing? Did you eat any of those squabs yet? We are getting lots of fresh fruit out and I've been having my fill of cantaloupe, plums, California grapes, peaches etc. Have we any grapes this year? Are you going to make wine Dad?

Well folks I have to close for now as I have a few more letters to dash off. Give my regards to everyone at home. Love to all.

July 24, 1945
San Francisco, Calif.

Dear Folks,

Hello everyone! Received all your letters this week and was very glad to hear from you again. You were right Mother I haven't any complaint in not getting any letters as it seems I've gotten one every day this week from you. I only wish I could write more often too, but going to boiler school I now go to classes from 8 o'clock until 4:30 in the afternoon so I haven't as much time to myself as before. My basketball shoes arrived on Saturday Mother and thanks also for sending me the Press and candy.

The weather has been warm and sunny this past week and today it was really hot, almost too hot to wear blues. I don't believe it has rained more than twice since I've been here. This is a pretty good school I'm going to and I've learned quite alot so far. Up to now we've studied boilers, economizer's, fuel oil systems and tanks and fireroom machinery.

Had the duty this past weekend so I didn't get a chance to go into town. Sunday afternoon I went down to #2 pool and got in some swimming. Just like going to the beach as two of the pools are filled with salt water. I believe I told you before about all the German prisoners we have here didn't I? You can see them all around during the day, digging ditches, gardening, washing windows etc. About 60 of them work up at the mess hall. You can tell the good treatment they receive as most of them are pretty big. Also you can notice how marching was drilled into them over there because when they march somewhere every one of them are in step without someone counting cadence.

So Bernie has finally left the state of Florida huh? Will you send me his address when you get it? Is Johnny Getz's ship out here? Haven't heard from Al lately. I received a letter from Carolyn (the girl in Mt. Holly) this week and she is going to Indiana University in September. Hank's girl in Mt. Holly, one of Carolyn's girlfriends, is going to the University of Delaware in Wilmington.

Has the deluge let up back East yet? I saw the damage it did in Phillipsburg in the newsreel this week. Did you kill any of your chickens yet Ma? I'll bet they're nice and big now. Drop me a line and let me know what you want in the line of clothes and towels etc. Hi Pete! Been down to the races at Garden State? Are you still in Paramount? Say Butz did that turtle arrive? How are the Cubs making out? Did you go to camp? Hello Dad. Did you wear my loud Hawaiian shirt to work? I'll have to close now as I have a little more writing to do. Give my regards to everyone at home. Love to you all.

July 30, 1945
San Francisco, Calif.

Dear Folks,

Received your letter of July 25th this morning and was very glad to hear from you. Also I received another Press, Bulletin and my basketball shoes arrived ok. How is everyone at home? Fine I hope. Glad to hear that the rainy weather you were having has cleared up. It has been rather chilly and damp the past few days, but on Friday it was swell out.

This week we are starting our third week at boiler school and I am learning quite a bit. We had a test at the end of last week and I got 97 or an A. This week we are studying safety valves, evaporators and air compressors. I had this past weekend off and Saturday night a couple of fellows and I went out to the Navy Mothers Club and had a big supper. Then we stayed for the dance and entertainment. One of the fellows had a birthday this week and they gave him a card and cake. On Sunday we took our first trip up to Chinatown, Nob Hill and Fisherman's Wharf.

Chinatown here is the largest other than in China itself. There are all kinds of Chinese shops and restaurants. Have you seen the picture called "Nob Hill"? It is the ritzy section of Frisco and also saw the classy Fairmount Hotel where President Truman stayed. Fisherman's Wharf is where the fishing fleet comes in with its daily catch. You can buy all sorts of fish at the sidewalks. We also dropped in to get some swell corn on the cob and it sure reminded me of good ole Jersey corn. This morning we had plums for breakfast and generally always have oranges, grapes or something.

I will try and get the towels and shorts for you Mother as soon as I have a chance to get to the stores. I think it would be best if you send the money by mail order in a letter. Well I must close for now as I have about six letters to answer. Give my regards to everyone at home. Love to all.

August 6, 1945
San Francisco, Calif.

Hello everyone. Received your letter of July 31 today and was very glad to hear from you again. Also received the Press that you sent air mail last week and I believe it arrived much quicker. Thanks alot for the fruit cake Mother. I rec'd it on Wednesday and some of the fellows and I had a swell midnight snack of it.

Well folks I haven't even been to sea yet and have already been on two ships. I'm now attached to the Richard B. Anderson (786), another destroyer. You see the Buck was originally supposed to be commissioned last March and already has had 3 crews assigned to it and broken up.

Now this past week the commission date was set back to Oct. 18th so they took the whole crew off the Buck and moved us to the Anderson which is supposed to be commissioned in Seattle on Sept. 15th. The way they are working on the Buck I guess it will never be commissioned. Tell Jim about my being on his ship ha! ha! Even after she is commissioned we will be out on a training cruise for 8 or 10 weeks. Boy! after reading about that new atomic bomb in tonight's paper and the damage it's supposed to do it doesn't look long before they will crack. Pretty soon they will have 1000 B-29 raids over Japan.

Last week who do I run into in the movie line on the base, but Joe Wigmore from Riverside. He is just recovering from a kidney operation. We shot the breeze about Riverside for a couple of hours. He was the one who was on that aircraft carrier that was hit. On Wednesday I rec'd a letter from Bernie and he is at Shoemaker, Calif., about 30 miles from here. He said he is waiting to ship out. I wrote and gave him the barracks phone number and told him to call me. I went on liberty Friday night and evidently he called and left a message for me to meet him at the Pepsi Cola Center in San Francisco. But they didn't deliver the message to me until Saturday afternoon so I missed him. However, with his being so close I hope we will have a chance to get together yet. We haven't seen each other since the day I came home from boot camp in October "42".

Haven't heard from Al, Skin or Hank for a couple of weeks. Had a letter from John, but he never says much. I never did get in touch with "Scotty" since I came back although I've intended to for some time. The weather in Frisco has been foggy, chilly and misty for the past two days. Last night it was just like an October night back home. I've been to quite a few places that had funny weather, but Frisco takes the cake. One day one can get a good tan out in the sun and the next it's cold enough for a peacoat.

How is the weather at home now? Still having lots of rain? Say Butz I'm sorry about your turtle not arriving. I saw the man I ordered it from in town on Friday night and he said the delay was caused by losing 5000 of them in some kind of accident when they were being shipped east. So maybe you'll get him yet. In the meantime I'm going to try and send you something else. When are you going to drop me another line?

How did you and the gang make out down at Egg Harbor Pete? Did you have a good time at Atlantic City? Guess it won't be long now until you start football practice huh? Mother what's happened to the Hartmans? I haven't had but one letter from them since I left. Has Jake arrived home? How did he get out? This Navy discharge plan is a joke. Skin wrote and said we would have to stay in 20 years to get enough points to get out ha! ha!

Hello Dad, how's your garden coming along? Do you have many grapes this year? Is the green beetle still moving? Well folks I have to close for now as I have a few more letters to dash off. Give my regards to everyone at home. Love to all.

August 14—V-J DAY. End of the war in the Pacific. Celebrations. Battle of Market Street in San Francisco.

August 14, 1945
San Francisco, Calif.

Dear Folks,

Hello everyone. How is everything at home? Fine, I hope. What do you think of the latest happenings? Ever since the dropping of the atomic bomb things have been happening thick and fast. Now it doesn't look like it will be too long before it is over for good.

I was abruptly awakened about 3 o'clock this morning with a coke bottle full of water thrown by a bunch of fellows who had just come in from liberty to tell me the war was over. The barracks was a mad house with fellows cheering and hollering. I'll bet the fellows out in the Fleet are really happy.

Even though it isn't official yet they really went wild in Frisco. (And me with the duty last night). Sailors and soldiers tore up bond booths and set them afire in the middle of Market Street. The fire company was called out, but couldn't get near enough to put it out as there were so many people. Then they started spinning a cable car around on the trolley table and finally pushed it off the tracks and a block up the street. When the police tried to break it up they started to take off with the police car.

It all ended up with a big parade forming and marching up and down Market Street. The radio said all the ships in Honolulu blew their whistles until they ran out of steam and Manila had just celebrated for the 3rd time. It just doesn't seem possible that it is going to end after so long. Now I hope it won't be long before they change over to a peace time basis and we may all be able to come home soon.

On Saturday we finished up our four weeks of boiler school and I got the highest mark on Saturday's test out of the nineteen in our class. Last week we studied the various effects in feed water on boilers and testing feed water for alkalinity, salinity and soap hardness. Monday I started on a week oxy-acetylene cutting and welding school. It is interesting and may prove useful sometime. Yesterday we cut up everything from ¼ inch steel plates to railroad rails.

The weather is cold enough to wear coats and gloves. It really has its changes, one day hot and the next day damp and foggy. This liquid sunshine they have is certainly something. Now that all this has come to a sudden ending I don't know whether they will put the Anderson in commission or not. So far it's scheduled to be commissioned on September 15th. But if we do I don't imagine we would go anywhere with everything all over. I guess it would be at least 5-6 months before they change over to a peace time schedule.

How is everything in Riverside? Has it been very hot? Well Pete and Butz it won't be long before you two will be going back to school huh? I know you'll like that and how! Are they starting to practice football yet Pete? If I stay here much longer I may be able to see some of the University of California games.

Hi Butz! I saw the fellows on Sunday about your turtle and he says they are just starting to send them out now. They were delayed because of floods. Are you still working at Banyas? (continued)

FLASH   FLASH   FLASH

August 14, 1945 4 o'clock (PCT)

THE WAR IS OVER

Just heard the above a few hours ago. The whole place is a madhouse. Hope I can get you on the phone tonight. Signing off for now. Love to all.

August 15–October 18–Quartered in barracks C awaiting the commission date of the USS Anderson.

August 18, 1945
San Francisco. Calif.

Dear Folks,

Hello everyone. It was sure good to hear your voice and talk to you again the other night. Just like I told you on the phone Mother, when I went back to my locker the letter you sent with the money order was there awaiting me.

Today (Sat.) I received another Press and a letter from Hartmans. Also rec'd letters from Skin, Hank and Bill Reilly, a fellow from Boston who is also on the Barton. I will try and get the shorts and towels off this week as I already have a box for them.

It still doesn't seem possible that the war is really over. Just wait until I send you the clippings and pictures of the celebration here in Frisco. They celebrated for four nights straight and it took police, shore patrol and Marines with bayonets to stop the rioting. There were bonfires in the middle of streets, trolley cars pushed off the tracks, sailors exchanging hats with officers and civilians (I got a woman marine's hat). The street was knee deep in paper. It started off with just celebrating, but wound up in a real riot. They rushed 600 shore patrol out of here in bus loads and Navy personnel out of Frisco for 72 hours until they cleaned up the city.

It looks as if I may be in for six or eight months according to this Navy Discharge Plan. They give you ½ point for every year of age and ½ point for every month in service and if married, 10 points. So in figuring it up I have 10 ½ pts. for age and 17 ½ for time in service. That gives me a total of 28 pts. and you need 44. So the way they have it now this will let out first all men who are in their late 30's and married. For example, there's a fellow here in the barracks who is 30 years old, married and has 2 ½ years in service, all of it in the States. He has enough points to get out. I have 3 yrs. in service, 20 yrs. old and 26 months of sea duty. In fact I have more points by the Army plan than I do the

Navy's. Because they give points for time overseas, engagements, time in service etc. So I guess all us young fellows will just have to wait until they lower the points. As the saying goes, it's all for the flag.

I'll bet the fellows out in the fleet are really glad now that it's ended. I imagine it won't be long before Skin will be coming back. Neither John, Al or I have enough points to get out right away. Skin told me indirectly that he is at Leyte in the Phillipines. Now that censorship has been lifted I guess they can say alot more now.

Are there many fellows home in Riverside now? It won't be long before the ole berg will be filling up again instead of steadily being deserted. Say Pete and Butz when are you two going to drop me a line? Haven't heard from you in months. Pete, Skin said he has written you several letters, but hasn't rec'd any answer. Have you started football practice? How are the Cubs making out Butz? Have you been camping anyplace? Did you have a good time at Atlantic City?

Mother it won't be long now before I'll be home to eat your good home cooking again. I'm really looking forward to it as I'm not the "picky" eater I used to be. Now I have a pretty big appetite. Since I've been back in the States that's my favorite past time, eating. Yesterday a couple of the fellows and I went over to Gym #2 and swam in the pool all afternoon. It has salt water in it and we really had an appetite worked up when we were finished.

Say Dad you won't have to worry about walking to work now that gas rationing is ended. You can start looking around for a new car as it won't be long until I'm home again, then we will get a good one. Well folks I must close for now as it's time to go to chow. Give my regards to everyone at home. Love to you all.

Aug. 22, 1945

Dear Mother,

Enclosed you will find 10 pairs of shorts and 5 towels. If you think they are all right I will send some more. If you have enough I will send you the balance of the money. I happened to have 4 pair of shorts size 30 that did not fit me so I will send them for Butz.

The light socket is the one that I told you about in one of my previous letters that I took off that Jap sub. It comes from the radio room and if you notice on the reverse side it was made in the U.S.A. (also piece of metal). The stone I picked up in the Rockies while coming through Colorado. The Women Marine Corps hat was captured in "The Battle of Market Street" in Frisco on the night when the war ended, Aug. 14, 1945. You will probably read in the clippings I am sending about wearing different hats.

August 22, 1945
San Francisco, Calif.

Dear Folks,

Hello everyone. I just thought I would drop you a few lines today as we engineers on the Anderson are going out tomorrow on a destroyer for a ten day training cruise. Most of the water tenders are wondering why they are sending us after already being on destroyers , but the main reason is to teach the firemen the ropes because most of them have never even seen a ship. I have five firemen under me who are supposed to be on my watch when we go out.

The commissioning date of the Anderson has been set back two more weeks until Sept. 29. So you can see how they are slowing up work on most of these ships since the war has ended. Most of the fellows don't think that it ever will go in commission now that everything is over. I received a letter from Skin and he said the fellows on the ship went wild when they heard that it ended. He said every ship in the harbor put on their big searchlights and lit up the sky. Then they fired rockets and flares for three hours straight.

The most popular topic of conversation around here isn't the weather or the war, but points, points, points. In our whole detail there are about two or three that have enough.

Fellows like Skin and I will just have to wait around until they get all the older married men discharged. Mother I went over to the small stores yesterday to get your 9 pair of shorts and 8 towels. I got a big surprise for it seems the service itself has also been hit by shortages. Now they only allow us 4 pair of shorts and one towel. I didn't know it until yesterday as I haven't been out there in some time.

However, I got a buddy of mine in front of me to get half and today I am going to go over again. I will try and get them sent before we go out on the training cruise. The bath towels are not as good as they used to be as you will notice in the material. I saw a good movie last night called "Wonder Man" and Count Basie and his Orchestra on the stage.

(continued Aug. 23). I sent your shorts and towels off yesterday afternoon Mother so you will receive them in 4 or 5 days. Have to close now as I've got to get them in the mail.

September 1, 1945
San Franciso, Calif.

Dear Folks,

Hello everyone. Just got in last night from a ten day cruise on the destroyer Haynesworth. Our whole crew went out and we water tenders showed the firemen how to stand a steaming match as the majority of them have never been to sea before. We went down off San Diego and fired torpedoes and guns and made a full power run coming back. What a time! If you wanted to see a bunch of seasick fellows you should have seen them. Most haven't been in the Navy more than 5 or 6 months and did they get sick. They kept me awake all night running for the bucket.

I even surprised myself by not getting sick even though I've been used to terra firma for the past six months. We even made them sicker by reminding them of greasy pork chops and raw oysters. Ha ! Ha! While aboard the Haynesworth I met fellows in their crew from Trenton, Camden, Perth Amboy, Scranton, Philadelphia and a fellow who used to work in Mt. Holly.

Rec'd all your letters this week, Mother's, Butz's and one from Vince yesterday. I rec'd the money order you sent me Mother just before we left on the cruise. Did you receive my packages I sent? So far the latest dope is that the Anderson will be commissioned on the 29th and we are to leave here for Seattle on the 25th. I'll get my sea pay back and will be able to save a little money before I'm discharged. It will be good to know that the ship will be for peace time use and not for war. Now that everything has ended things are slowing up and I imagine the filling out and shakedown cruise will take from 10-12 weeks.

As far as I know I am the only one who has come off a 2200 destroyer like the Barton and it will be just like the Barton again. There has certainly been lots of good news in the paper the past few days for the Navy. The Secretary of the Navy announced that they will give points for overseas duty and also released a schedule for discharges. They plan to release 835,000 men by January 1 or about 235,000 per month. Boy! I sure hope I'm one of them.

Last night I heard on the radio the surrender ceremonies held aboard the Missouri in Tokyo Bay and the speech by the President. It seems to me as if I just enlisted last year and this war was one big bad dream. Guess what? I rec'd a letter from Bernie and he's over in Oakland. He's been assigned to the LSD-6 or landing ship dry dock. I have the duty this weekend, but Monday being Labor Day we had a holiday and 0900 liberty in the morning. As we also expect to be here until the 15th or later it looks as if we will finally see each other. I'm afraid he'll wind up at some South Pacific Island as he hasn't had any sea duty and won't have enough points.

Did you have a nice time down at Avalon and Atlantic City? I guess there are lots of people around now huh? Rec'd a letter from Carolyn and she has been down to Beach Haven. On Saturday she said the wind was howling and there were high waves. She is leaving to attend the University of Indiana sometime this month. Also heard from Al and he talks as if he may be back in soon. Haven't heard from Skin, John or Hank lately.

Thanks for your nice long letter Butz. I'm glad to hear that your turtle arrived at last. Where are you keeping it? Boy! you sure have been traveling around alot during your summer vacation. When do you start school? Hi Vince! thanks for your interesting letter. Riverside is really gifted with havin good coaches, first Pappas, Diesend and now Wistert. I can still remember when he played with Michigan. The University of California opens their season with St. Mary's Pre-Flight on the 22nd so I hope I get to see the game although I hope I am able to get home in time to see you play before the season ends. So Polino is going to Shoemaker. Sounds kinda bad for him as generally they are either assigned to a ship there like Bernie or sent out to the islands as fleet replacements. But you know how old Polino is, I guess it won't make much difference to him. When school opens tell the "Chief" I said hello and to keep 224 on the ball.

Do you think you will need any more towels or shorts Mother? It seems as if all the fellows are buying them to send home as I saw several of them wrapping them. I also think I'll ship a mattress I have before I leave for Seattle as I have two of them since I came back. When I come home Mother you won't find me particular about what I eat like I used to be as now I eat everything. I'm looking forward to your swell home cooked meals again. Myself and many others have found out by being away from home during the war just how much you appreciate your home, your parents and all the other things you had before the war.

Hi ! Dad. I guess you feel pretty "ritzy" now riding around in the car with a radio playing. (That is when Vince will let you have the car) ha! ha! I suppose it feels good to be back to peacetime working hours now huh? Say Dad when you see Faunce will you see if we can get a new bellows now for the camera? I see in the paper where they lifted the ban on film and as soon as we are able to take cameras aboard ship I am going to try and take as many as possible before I get out.

September 6, 1945
San Francisco, Calif.

Dear Folks,

Yesterday I rec'd your letter and Press's of the 30th. Thanks for sending them Mother as I really enjoyed having some of the home town news again. After three years Bernie (the Greek I call him) and I finally met. And just as I bumped intoAl in the Golden Gate Theatre I met Bernie in the ice skating rink in Berkley. Ever since he's been here in Calif. we have been trying to arrange a meeting place, but kept missing each other. All at once we bump into each other by accident.

Boy! were we glad to see each other. We talked over old times for hours and have been out together almost every night this week. He isn't supposed to leave until October 5 so we will have lots of time together. He told me all about his girl he's engaged to from Florida and from his pictures seems to be a nice girl.

Bernie still talks about the good time we had camping at Burlington and even though we all wound up with ivy poison he still wants to go up again after we get back home. Has the weather still been very warm? The past three days have been the hottest I've seen it here yet. To top that off they are holding a victory parade in Frisco on Sunday and our whole detail has been elected to march in it. Every morning and afternoon we have been drilling with leggings, guard belts and rifles. Now I know how the Army and West Point cadets feel because by the time we get back to the barracks we are soaked from sweating and our feet feel like lead weights. It really does look nice when we all march and go through the manual of arms together.

Have you seen Lester Yearly? I guess there are lots of fellows arriving home now. It just will be a matter of time for me as I hear they are to release the new Navy discharge system soon. I'm glad you're pleased with the things I sent Mother. After this marching and parade affair is over I will try to get to the small stores and get some more for you. Sure had a good laugh about Butz's turtle crawling all the way into the living room. Since Spottie is jealous I'll bet he would swallow him if he had the chance. Have Pete and Butz started school yet?

Well folks I'll have to make this rather short and sign off for now as it's time to put my leggings on and fall out. Give my regards to everyone at home. Love to all of you.

September 9, 1945
San Francisco, Calif.

Dear Mother,

I received your very nice long letter on Friday and was very glad to hear from you again. The mail seems to be coming quicker now as I received it in three days. I'm glad to hear that you had such an enjoyable time with the Lenahans on Labor Day. I guess I won't ever forget that day either as that was the day I ran into Bernie. We have already been out 3 or 4 nights together and as we both said it's just like old times. On Monday I also had another pleasant surprise. I received a letter from Al and he's out in the bay again.

Just finished dropping a few lines and if all three of us can get together we will really have a swell reunion. Al said that they expect to decommission their ship this month. Sure hope Skin can get back to the states soon, then we will really celebrate as I haven't seen him in two years. Mother I guess you have been wondering why I am writing this letter to you. Well I received a letter from Carolyn this week and she said she would very much like to meet you before she leaves for college this month and wondered if it was alright with me. She mentioned that she might call you. I would like you to meet her as I think she's swell and I know you will like her too.

As I told her also I wanted to bring her home and introduce her personally to you and Dad when I was home on leave, but it seemed like there was always something else popping up. Now don't think I'm going to get engaged or anything like that as I don't plan to settle down just yet and I still have hopes of going to college after I'm out. It's just that I'd like you and Carolyn to know each other so you can tell me what you think she's like. (If you two women get together, don't tell her any of my secrets, Ha! Ha!).

I will try to get some more towels and if you need any blankets I'm pretty sure they are $8.50. The blankets are just like the one's you washed for me when I was home. However I would like you to send me $20 by money order when you receive this letter as I am about down to my last dollar. I know you must think that I'm always sending for money, but losing $16 by not getting sea pay and only $11 every two weeks keeps me pretty low. You see, when I was on the ship I was drawing $26 per pay day instead of $11 besides the $50 going home. I only used to go out 2 or 3 nights a week, but since I bumped into Bernie I have been going out almost every night.

Hope it won't be too long until they straighten out this Navy discharge point system, then I'll be able to come home and start earning some money. I must close for now Mother as it's about time for lights out. Will write more about the big parade tomorrow. Until then, with all my love.

September 10, 1945
San Francisco, Calif.

Dear Folks,

At present I'm on watch in the detail office and have the 10PM to 2AM P.O. watch so I'm taking time out to drop you a few lines. As you will see by the enclosed news clippings yesterday's big parade was quite an event here in Frisco. Our whole detail paraded in our dress blues, leggings, guard belts and rifles. The parade started promptly at 12:30 and the last contingent passed the reviewing stand at 3:30. We really drew a big ovation from the crowd as we passed up Market Street. Was it hot! We had to march about 16 or 18 blocks and by the time we were through we were about wet from sweating. We finished by passing in review in front of General Wainwright on the reviewing stand. In all it was a big parade with thousands of people lining both sides of the street.

Up until now we are still scheduled to leave for Seattle about the 25th of this month. Yesterday they finally released the point system giving ¼ point for each month of sea duty. With alot of figuring I find myself to have 34 points as of this month. Now if I had only taken out a dependency allotment before this, instead of a voluntary $50 allotment would have the additional 10 points to make 44. As it is I'll just have to wait until they reduce the critical score which is supposed to be about November 1. In the meantime I still gain ½ point per month for time in service. I imagine I will make it by the first of the year at least because they will start dropping the points as the months go by. Today I saw a bunch of fellows coming out of the personnel office with their honorable discharges. Boy! you should have seen the smiles and happy faces.

Just received two more Press's today and it was sure swell to read some more news from home. I guess Riverside will start to liven up now that some of the fellows are starting to return. Well folks I'm not going to write much in this letter as I want to enclose some clippings in the envelope. I have a pretty lot of them, but will send some a little later as they are too big to put in one envelope. Hoping to hear from you soon again I remain with love to all of you.

September 15, 1945
San Francisco, Calif.

Dear Folks,

Hello everyone. I haven't received any letters from you this week, but two Press's arrived yesterday dated the 11th. The mail seems to be coming quicker now as it took them just 4 days and letters are taking two to three days.

I guess you've received my letters telling of the big parade we had here. We were commended on our marching by the admiral of the 12th Naval District. Mother do you want any blankets from the small stores? I think I told you in one of my previous letters that they were $8.25. If I had enough money I would send them. You see, next Tuesday the 18th until Saturday the 20th we leave for Seattle. I won't have too much time left to get them off.

How is the weather at home? It has been cold enough the past two days to wear peacoats and gloves. Did you read about the big bunch that arrived here on the Saratoga? Most of them were sent to Treasure Island to be reclassified and given leave and did they look cold after being used to the tropical climate. The latest dope is that we are to put the ship in commission on the 29th and have about a 12 week shakedown cruise which should run well into December. Before they leave the states the crew is to be cut down from 360 to a peacetime complement of about 180 men. By that time the points should be dropped and I should have enough. Wouldn't it be swell to be discharged and get home for Christmas and the New Year?

I certainly consider myself lucky to have been in the states this long and been here for the ending of the war. On Thursday I was on my way over to the laundry and I bumped into a gunner mate who had just been transferred from the Barton out in Guam. He told me several things that Hank could not tell me in his letters due to censorship. He said the Barton was rammed by the destroyer Ingraham 65 miles off Tokyo during the battle of Okinawa and lost 40 feet of her bow. Luckily no one was killed. Also, the chief gunners mate died of burns when a white phosphorous shell exploded in mount 2. He said at Iwo Jima they sank two surface ships and got four planes at Okinawa. You can see that they've been through alot since I left. Hank will be able to tell me lots more when they get back to the states.

Say Pete and Butz how do you like getting back to the school routine? How are your turtles doing Butz? How are the Cubs getting along? What kind of a team are they having this year Pete? Who's scheduled for the first game?

Dad did you see Faunce about the camera yet? If I can I'm going to try and get some shots of the ship. Mother are the Hartman girls still around? I still haven't any answer from my letters. Well I must close for now folks as it's about time for taps. Hoping this letter finds all you all in good health. Give my regards to everyone at home.

P.S. Enclosed is a picture Hank sent me of the Fireroom Gang of the Barton.

September 24, 1945
San Francisco, Calif.

Dear Folks,

This is my first chance to do any writing as we just got back in Saturday. We were out on the USS Norris for a week of gunnery practice, firing torpedoes and speed runs. We didn't do too bad this trip and only a few of the fellows got sick. Now I hear we are to go out for two more weeks next Monday. I suppose they figure we are just sitting around the barracks waiting for our ship so they send us out on a ship in here. The Norris has been in commission only ten weeks and is a little longer than the Barton. It is even equipped with an ice cream and soda fountain which is saying alot for a destroyer.

I rec'd your two letters, money order and lovely card when I came back to the barracks Mother. This week I will try to send those other towels off. I guess you won't be able to use these Navy blankets as I don't think they would even be big enough for my bed in the old room. We have small mattresses and they just about cover us. Is Spottie any better? What did he swallow? I hope that by the time you receive this letter that he will be ok. Do you still have the turtle Butz? How are your Cubs doing?

Say Pete how did you make out on Saturday's game? Who did you play? Will you drop me a few lines and let me know the latest dope on the team? We got off the ship too late on Saturday to see the game between St. Mary's and the Univeristy of California. But yesterday I saw a swell game at Kezar Stadium in Frisco between the Fleet City Bluejackets and the 2nd Air Force Superbombers. Of course, the sailors won 7-0. Some of the former college stars that played were Frank Sinkwich of Georgia, Lou Zonteni, Bill Riffle and Steve Juzwich of Notre Dame, Paul Christman of Missouri and Kahman of Temple. I'll send you the program. Who is playing with the Turner's team? It sure seems funny to watch a football game in California as it was so hot yesterday we were sweating with our blues on. I was used to going to the games at home and stomping your feet to keep warm.

Did you find anything out about the camera Dad? When we were out on the Norris alot of fellows had cameras taking pictures of torpedoes being fired and lots of other swell shots. They just put out a notice to all commanding officers about letting pictures of ships to be taken. I believe there's still some film for it in one of the bureau drawers in the dining room. This afternoon a few of the fellows and I went over to the pool for a swim. It was an exceptionally hot day so we went out on the sun deck. Between that sun at the ball game and now today I'm getting brown again.

Treasure Island is getting pretty crowded now that so many are coming in every day to be discharged. They have #1 gym full of bunks to accommodate them all. It's not unusual to see a chow line about as long as from our house to Jimmie's and that's not exaggerating. Did you read in the paper about the 3rd Fleet coming in here on Oct. 10th in New York for Navy Day on the 25th? There are supposed to be about 24 big battleships and cruisers. They are bringing back 7000 passengers to be discharged. You can see just how crowded it will be in Frisco when they get here. Well folks I'll have to close now as it's close to 10 PM and time for taps. Give my regards to everyone at home. Hoping to hear from you soon again. I remain with love to all of you.

P.S. Enclosed you will find a recent picture of Carolyn which she sent to me. Will you send it back in your next letter as I am going to have an enlargement of it made.

October 4, 1945
Aboard the USS Norris

Dear Folks,

Hello everyone. We just came back to Treasuure Island after going out on Sunday morning. Today they brought our mail aboard and I received your letter of the 27th. On Monday and Tuesday we had gunnery practice firing during the day and at night. Wednesday it was so foggy you couldn't see 50 yards ahead so we just cruised around and came in this morning. Then we had to fuel the ship and take on ammunition. Tomorrow we are supposed to get underway for torpedo firing.

I'm glad you can get some blankets Mother at that price as they are cheaper than at the small stores. At the barracks I have 5 more bath towels and those shirts for Butz. I'll get them off as soon as I get off here and also am going to try to send home my mattress as the government is supposed to take over all mattresses on the 15th.

I certainly was sorry to hear about "Spottie". I'll miss him. Where did you get the new dog so soon? Say Pete, I want to congratulate you on being made captain of the team. That's swell and here's hoping you win all of the games. I only wish I could be home to see you play a couple of games. When you get the chance write and let me know all about the team and the games.

Last Saturday another fellow and I went out to Berkley and saw the game between the University of California and the University of Southern California. Cal won 13-2. On Saturday night we saw "Louie" Armstrong and his band at the Golden Gate. On Friday who walked into the barracks again but Bernie. We haven't seen each other for two weeks as he was going to school at Mare Island. We went out together on Friday night. He said they expect to leave for Seattle on the 9th and we are to go up on the 15th so it looks as if we will be able to see each other up there also. Yesterday I received a letter from Skin telling me they were going to Jensun, Korea. It looks as if they're going out farther now even though the war's over. However, he said that they will have their 18 months out there in November so he said there is talk they may be back by the first of the year. We two will sure have some celebrating to do when we see each other again.

Well folks tomorrow I will have exactly 3 years to the day in the Navy. Gee, it hardly seems that long at all. Now I hope it won't be too long before I'm out. I saw a schedule of points and months for release today and according to my 35 points I should be able to get out sometime in January. Dad, if my camera can't be fixed I'll try to borrow one of the fellows. But if you can see if you could pick up some film size 620. One of the fellows has a camera that uses that size and he will let me use that if I can get some film.

When you go to New York on Navy Day you will really see the big ships that have given the Japs all the trouble during the war. Maybe you will even have a chance to go aboard one. Here's some good news that will interest you. The other night I was reading in the paper about the 87 units of the 3rd Fleet that are to arrive on the West Coast and those going to New York. The Barton is coming back with them and is due to arrive at Everett, Washington some time this month. In fact, our whole squadron 60 is coming back, the O'Brien, Walke, Sumner and Mansfield. Boy! I'd give anything to see them when they dock, will they be happy. I may even get up to Washington as I understand Everett isn't too far from Seattle.

Mother I wouldn't call up Mrs. Ibbitson as I haven't heard from Hank in about 6-8 weeks myself and I kinda think he's going to surprise them by sending a telegram or something when they arrive. Have you seen it in the paper yet? Ma you will probably receive a picture some time this month which I bought and am sending C.O.D. It is a picture in a nice frame of a 2200 destroyer exactly like the Barton and the Anderson. Under the picture it has my name and campaign bars and the planes and ships the destroyer is credited with. Please take the money out of my check when it arrives. Also, please send me $15 by M.O. and I hope this will be the last time I'll have to send for money. On

Sunday we get to Seattle and I'll start drawing sea pay again when the Anderson goes into commission.

Hello Butz, when are you going to drop me a few lines? Do you still have your turtles? How are the Cubs making out? I received literature this week that I've sent for from the University of Notre Dame, Drexel Institute of Technology and Rutgers. According to most of the entrance requirements I'll have to pick up some geometry as I didn't take any in high school. Just received the Press you sent on the 27th Ma and sure enjoyed its contents. Also received a letter from Johnny Wilhelm saying he just got back from a 15 day leave at home.

Well I'll have to sign off now hoping to hear from you soon again. Give my regards to everyone at home. Love to you all.

October 10, 1945
Aboard USS Norris

Dear Folks,

Hello everyone. I'm writing this letter aboard the Norris and at present we are at anchor in the bay. This is the first opportunity I have had to answer your letter which I received on Saturday when we came in for the weekend

Last week and this week we have been operating a couple hundred miles off the coast having AA firing, night firing and making torpedo runs. Most of this wek it has been foggy and today was the first time I saw it rain since we came in to Frisco last March. I guess the rainy season is just starting. Due to the fog we couldn't do any firing so we came in this afternoon.

We are supposed to get off here on Friday and leave for Seattle on Monday or Tuesday. The ship is due to be commissioned on the 19th or 20th. I'm sure disappointed Pete that I can't get home this year to see you play. How is your leg now? Did you get in the game against Moorestown on Saturday? Write and let me know how you made out huh?

As we came in on Saturday afternoon I was just in time to get to the game in Berkley and see California play Washington. It was a swell game with Cal winning 27-14. On Sunday I saw a WOW of a game, St. Mary's playing the Univeristy of Nevada. Right now St. Mary's is the hottest team on the west coast winning three straight games. They beat Nevada 39-0. St. Mary's scored on the second play of the game in one of the most beautiful plays I've ever seen. It started out as an end run and developed into a triple lateral with the 3rd man running 74 yards for the score. In the first six minutes of the game the score was 14-0. Maybe you've already heard of the future All-American they have, "Herm" Weidemeyer and his running mate, Spike Condero. They are both Hawaiians from Honolulu. Say Butz how's our new dog? Are you teaching him any tricks like "Spottie" used to do? Is he a good watch dog? Where did you get him from?

(Oct. 12th continued) Sorry I wasn't able to finish this letter on Wednesday, but I had to go on watch and went out yesterday and just got back in again tonight. Yesterday I received your letter and money order and two Press's. The ole home paper sure looked good and I enjoyed its contents, especially about the fellows at home and the RHS and Turners teams.

Yesterday and today it was rather cloudy and we only fired two torpedoes this morning and came back in. While we were off the coast we ran into five big whales, all of them diving and spouting. More and more transports full of soldiers and sailors arriving from the Pacific are coming in here every day.

As you come under the Golden Gate Bridge you see a large sign on the side of the mountain which reads "WELCOME HOME WELL DONE". It's in big white letters and at night it is all lit up. When the third fleet arrives on Monday there will certainly be some wild cheering as they go under the bridge. I still remember the night when we came in. We made so much noise it almost caused the bridge to collapse. Are you still planning on going up to New York on Navy Day to see the ships? Has the picture of the destroyer arrived yet Mother?

We are getting off tomorrow and leave for Seattle on Monday the 15th. The commission date of the ship has been put back a week until the 26th now so maybe we will be in a barracks up there for awhile. Also, I hear the complement is being lowered too, so instead of having 365 men we will have 235. I'll write to you again when we get to Seattle. Must close for now as I want to drop a few lines to Skin. Give my regards to everyone at home. Sending my love to you all.

October 15, 1945
San Francisco, Calif.

Dear Folks,

Just a few lines to let you know that we are leaving for Seattle. We were up bright and early at 6 o'clock this morning to pack sea bags and lash up our hammocks. Our gear was loaded on the trucks at 2 o'clock this afternoon and now we are just sitting around waiting to leave. Our train is due to leave Oakland at 9:30 tonight so I suppose we will arrive up there on Wednesday or Thursday.

We will be in the barracks for a few days as the commission date is October 26. The weather this week has been rather foggy and overcast and it rained a little this morning. I have my peacoat packed on top as I hear Washington is cold. Admiral Bull Halsey's third fleet came under the Golden Gate Bridge at noon today and I could hear the horns and sirens all the way up to the barracks. Everett, Washington is only about 35 miles from Seattle so when we get up there I may have a good chance of seeing the Barton when she comes in this month. Had a letter from one of the fellows there and he said several of the fellows had already left on points and some transferred.

Yesterday I received Pete's letter and today received Mother's letter of the 11th. Also received the two Press's you sent. Glad to hear about your beating Moorestown Pete. How did you do against Bristol? On Saturday I saw St. Mary's trounce College of the Pacific 61-0. I sent you some of the programs this week. Is Chief Triebels back this year?

Hi! Butz, how do you like being back to school? Do you still take care of the chickens and pigeons? You can let them out to fly and give them a bath when you have the chance. You can let them all fly as they should be used to the coop by now. Mother I sent a box on Saturday and you should receive it any day. I sent five more large towels and shirts for Butz. After trying for two years I finally got hold of a foul weather jacket and can use it when I get out. The sweatshirt is too small for me so maybe Pete or Butz can wear it.

Hi! Dad how's everything going with you? It must seem funny to be working on watches again now huh? Do you still work on the lathe? Have you seen any football games this year? Is the green beetle still holding up? When I get home we'll see if we can't get hold of a new one. Couldn't Faunce fix the camera or does it have to be sent to the company? I have a couple rolls of 620 film and one of the fellows is going to loan me his camera so I should be able to get some shots when we get up to Seattle. Well folks I'll have to close for now as we have to go out to "chow". I'll write again when I get to Seattle. Give my regards to everyone at home. With love to all of you.

October 18, 1945
Seattle, Washington

Dear Folks,

Hello everyone. Just a few lines to let you know that I'm way up here in this northern state of Washington. We left Frisco 2 o'clock Tuesday morning after waiting for the train since 9:30 and arrived here in Seattle at 3 o'clock Wednesday afternoon. We had day coaches on the train coming up and our whole detail of 300 men had the train to ourselves.

Jim was right when he said that it was nice scenery. On the way up we passed through Oregon and into Washington and the scenery was really beautiful. After leaving California we started to climb the mountains and picked up another locomotive to take us up and over them. Here you could see snow capped moutains covered with big spruce, cedar and pine trees, running trout streams and every so often a clear blue lake. The climate reminds me of Jersey in October. It's clear and brisk and with the appetite it gives you, you feel like eating a whole cow. After leaving California the temperature was in the high 70's and coming up here where it's in the 30's is really a change.

However, I like it here much better than Calif. because I like this sort of climate. Most of us slept with two blankets on last night and it was so cold this morning we hated to get out of bed. At present we are temporarily based in a barracks until next Friday the 26th when we will move down to the ship and put it in commission. Today we met the rest of the officers and chiefs and they seem to be a pretty good bunch. Next Wednesday the 24th we are going to have our ship's party in the Moose Hall in Seattle.

It's going to cost us $4 and it looks like I'll have to bother you again Mother. We aren't to be paid until November 1 so I'll need about $10 (and no more) to hold me till then. I hate to be bothering you all the time by sending for money, but until I start drawing sea pay which will be the day we're commissioned. Now that I have the chance to get around like this I'd just have to sit around in the barracks waiting for payday.

When we left on Monday night we saw the battleships of the 3rd Fleet anchored in the bay and all of them were lighting up the sky with their big search lights. It looked nice and just like they used to do when the fleet came in port during peace time. Most of the fleet units are arriving along the West Coast from San Diego to Seattle. Some time next week I'm going to try and go out to Everett to see if the Barton is in just yet.

How is everything at home? Has there been any snow? Is it very cold? Are there many fellows back in town now? Did you beat Bristol on Saturday Pete? Who are you playing on Thanksgiving Day? Did you see any of Penn's games? Mother did you receive that box I sent yet? I sure hope I'll be able to get home for Christmas or New Year's so I can have one of your good meals again. I can't wait to get some of that good chicken.

Hi! Butz. I know I'm a little late, but I want to wish you a "Happy Birthday". Have you received the card I sent? Hello Dad, have you gotten out your long underwear yet? I suppose it won't be long before the storm windows go up huh? Well I'll sign off for now. Give my regards to everyone at home. I remain with love to all of you.

October 20–Left for Seattle, Washington.

October 22–Arrived at the Harbor Island Navy Base in Seattle, Washington.

October 26–USS Richard B. Anderson (DD 786). Commissioned at the Todd Pacific Ship yard this date at 1030.

October 26, 1945
USS Anderson
Seattle

Dear Folks,

Today I received your letter of the 22nd and was very glad to hear from you as it was the first one I received since leaving California. This morning at 10:45 the Anderson was commissioned. The Captain accepted the ship from the representatives of the Todd Ship Building Yard and the flag and commission pennant were run up. A band played music for the ceremonies and there were photographs aboard to take pictures. I wish you could have been here as we could escort guests through the ship.

Our first meal was supper and they really got off to a good start. We had steak, sweet potatoes, lettuce salad, corn, ice cream, pie, cupcakes and fresh milk. I only hope they continue to feed that good. But Mother they can never beat your good Sunday chicken dinners.

The Anderson is the same type destroyer as the Barton, but a little bigger and has more room. We have a pretty good crew and the Captain is a sweet fellow. It seems funny living aboard ship again after being in the barracks for the past couple months. Of all the places I've visited I believe Seattle is one of the nicest. The people are sociable and swell to the sailors. There are lots of scenic points of interest and always something to do. During Navy Week they are having a dance every night at the Armory and hostesses to dance with the sailors. Tomorrow on Navy Day they are planning a big celebration and at night the fleet is going to light up the harbor with their searchlights. Our ship is even going to be all dressed up with the different colored flags.

On Monday night I went to an ice hockey game between Seattle and the Westminster Royals from Canada. It was the first ice hockey game I've ever seen and it is really a fast and rough sport. Last night a couple of the fellows and I went to the dance out at the Civic Auditorium. Last Tuesday night I went out to Everett on the bus. After leaving the bus terminal I hadn't walked a half block and who do I bump into but Hank and a bunch of the old gang. You should have seen the back slapping that went on then. We spent a good time that night together talking over old times. The Barton and a submarine are in at Everett for Navy Day, then they are going down to the Los Angeles Navy Yard for repairs. Then all of the crew is supposed to get a 38 day leave.

Boy! now I'm glad that I was transferred last February. After I left they hit Iwo Jima, Okinawa and Tokyo. They shot down 10 Jap planes, sunk a sub, was hit by another kamikaze, rammed by another destroyer and lost 40 feet of their bow. On the way back to the states they rode into a typhoon and took a 60 degree roll. You can see what experiences they went through. I hope I will have the chance to see them again before they leave here.

Thanks for sending me the $10 Mother and the stamps. Make sure you take it from my check and not your own money now. If you send stamps again you can send 6 cents air mail as we have a fleet P.O. address and can send them for 6 cents. Must close for now folks as it's almost time for taps. Give my regards to everyone at home. Sending my love to all of you I remain—your loving son and brother.

October 27 -31 —Loaded stoves.

November 2, 1945
Seattle

Dear Folks,

Hello everyone. By now I suppose you have been wondering why I haven't written recently. Since the day we were commissioned we have been kept busy working loading supplies, stoves and ammunition. I haven't had much chance to do any writing. I've just finished washing some clothes and at present am on watch here in the aft fireroom.

After the commissioning we went out in the sound for a trial run then picked up our torpedoes and loaded ammunition all day Friday. The scenery in Washington, and all along Puget Sount, is really beautiful. It is just like going up the Delaware, but here it is mountains on either side covered with tall spruce, pine and fir trees. Lots of cottages and cabins dot the shoreline and the hunting and fishing here is excellent. In all I think this state is one of the nicest I've seen yet.

Yesterday we went out for the day to calibrate our radar and gyro compass. Tomorrow we are to go out and fire all the guns for the first time. We will be around Seattle making trial runs until the 9th and then leave for San Diego where we are due to arrive on the 12th. Then we will have a seven week shakedown cruise and come back up to Seattle. We have a good skipper and a good crew and so far are getting pretty good eats.

During the course of writing this letter I was interrupted by someone coming down the ladder. You couldn't guess who it was. Bernie. At the beginning of this week I received a letter from him saying that they were coming here to Seattle. But whoever expected his ship to be tied up right in back of us and neither of us knowing that our ships were so close together. They came in yesterday morning and we pulled in front of them in the afternoon. He said he happened to be looking at the ship and recognized the name on the fantail. Also, he said they expect to go to San Diego soon too so it looks as if we are following each other up and down the coast. This week received all your letters, Mother's, Butz's and Dad's and was glad to hear from you again. Also received one from Skin and now he's in China. He certainly is getting his share of moving around even though the war has ended.

He made MOMM 2/c too so he is really doing all right by himself. After or during our shakedown I have hopes and a fairly good chance of making WT 2/c myself, so here's hoping I'm in charge of Section 3 in the forward fireroom which rates second class. How did you enjoy seeing the fleet on Navy Day? I heard the ceremonies over the radio. I'll bet it really shook New York when they fired that 21 gun salute for the President. Say Pete, how did the team do against Burlington and Mount Holly? Sure wish I could get home to see you play a couple of games. Will you send me the write up on the games?

Last week being Navy Week they really treated we sailors swell here in Seattle. Every night a Navy Dance was held at the armory and a formal was held on Saturday night. Lots of the fellows received invitations to dinner at homes, free tickets to football and ice hockey games. The other night I saw Seattle play the Vancouver Canucks from Canada in a fast hockey game. Well folks I must close for now so I can get this in the mail. Hoping this letter finds all of you fine and in good health. Give my regards to everyone at home. I remain with love to all of you.

November 1-9–We went out into Puget Sound for trial runs. We calibrated loaded ammunition and torpedoes with depth charges.

November 10–Left Seattle for a 7 week shakedown to San Diego.

November 12–Arrived in San Diego, California and had a commander's inspection of the ship.

November 13–We stayed in port.

November 13-17–Operated with a submarine.

November 13, 1945
San Diego, Calif.

Dear Folks,

By now I hope you have received my previous letter in which I enclosed a photographic clipping of the commissioning. I suppose you have them wondering why you haven't heard from me so often and are probably wondering what has become of me. Now that I'm aboard ship again I haven't as much time to write as I did at Treasure Island because we are kept pretty busy. However, I will try and write whenever I can and let you know what I'm doing.

Since you last heard from me we have left Seattle and are now in San Diego. We left last Friday and arrived yesterday the 12th. It snowed the last two days we were in Seattle and really got cold. Now arriving here in sunny Southern California is quite a change.

The first day out of Seattle we ran into an 18 hour storm and a rough sea with high waves. Once again in my Navy career I got seasick. The officers, chiefs and half the crew were sick and running around with a pale green palor. To think that I was just getting used to land once again after being on Treasure Island for so long. You should have seen the long chow line that formed after we arrived here, it was almost the length of the ship. Boy! everyone started to eat again.

The following day turned out clear with a blue sky overhead and the sea running in lazy ground swells. On the way down we made a four bow speed run with all four boilers. It was the first time she ran wide open and made 34.8 knots. The Barton made 36 knots, but the Barton was of the 2200 class and this one displaces 2900 tons. When we were going free ahead they pulled a crash astern from full ahead to full astern. She vibrated like a Mexican jumping bean and the water really poured over the stern. The speed run was made mainly to test the ship for vibrations at full speed. We had several vibrations and experts aboard with instruments to record the vibrations at high speed.

Last night we arrived about 5 o'clock and have been tied up to a buoy all day. Today we stood inspection by the captain of the destroyer base. We are supposed to be here for several weeks shakedown which will run into January. It is just like the one we had in Bermuda on the Barton— go out for a few days operating with subs, gunnery practice, torpedo firing, speed trials and squadron maneuvers. If we should be here during the holidays I hope that they give us leave for Christmas or over New

Year's. The way I have it figured as far as points go, I should get out sometime in February. At the end of this month I will have 35 ¾ points and in February I'll have 37. On December 1 it drops to 39 for discharge so if they continue to drop I should get out by then.

Well folks how is everything at home? Have you had much cold weather or snow yet? It seems as if I always strike it right for the past three winters I've always been in the warm climates. I've only seen snow twice in the past two years. Pete how is the team making out? How did you do against Burlington, Mt. Holly and Florence? I sure hope you beat Mt. Holly or I'm in for a razzing. Have you seen any more college games? Say Pete is the "Chief" still at 224? Hi! there Butz how are you making out? I just bet you are getting your sled ready to go huh? How is your new Spottie making out, did you teach him any tricks? How do you like being a full fledged Scout now?

Hello Mother how are your chickens doing, are you getting many eggs? I'm really looking forward to one of your good chicken dinners when I come home. And gee! do I miss your chocolate cakes and pies. Will you send me some more Press's? Has the framed picture of the destroyer arrived yet? I had it sent C.O.D. so when it comes be sure to take it out of my check. Has Ernie or Bill Seiler hit the states yet? Where is Letch and Lawrence Yearly now–does Ray Clauss, the "shallow water sailor" still get home? Received a letter from Skin and he was telling me about the 48 hour liberty he spent in Tiensten, China. He's certainly getting around quite a bit since the war ended hasn't he? He told me the exchange rate is $3000 Chinese to $1 American money. Have you heard from John lately? Haven't heard from him or Al in quite some time.

Hello Dad are you still seeing the football games? That Army-Navy game this year is going to be a real scrap with both going undefeated in six games. How is the Turner team doing? Are you still working six days a week? Say Dad did my camera come back yet? I borrowed a 620 Kodak from one of the fellows and got several good shots of the commissioning, the ship underway, shots of us going under the Golden Gate Bridge and shots of some of the gang. I only hope they turn out OK. We are getting them developed this week and I will send you some.

Well folks I guess that's all for now as I'm beginning to get writer's cramp so I'd better close. Give my regards to everyone at home. I am with love to you all.

November 17-December 12–Operating with the USS Thompson holding battle practice and night training, target and AA firing, torpedo runs, drills, etc.

November 20, 1945
At Sea in the Pacific

Dear Folks,

Received your long 3 section letter the other day and was very glad to hear from you again and to learn all the up to date news. Was glad to hear that you had such an enjoyable trip up to North Jersey and a good close up view of the fleet. I certainly wish I could have been home when the "gang" was there. I can just picture John and Jim putting on that show. What did they try to drink, Torpedo Alcohol? Ha! Ha!

All this past week we have been out for 5" target firing, AA firing and today we are making practice torpedo runs with other destroyers. This shakedown always keeps you busy going to GQ, fire drills, collision drills, abandon ship drills, etc. Last night when we came in I washed out some clothes and went to bed early for a change. I send all my dungarees to the ship's laundry, but wash my own whites. I generally have a hard time trying to keep my shorts white as I'm always bumping against a wall in the fireroom and getting fuel oil on them. When I get out I'm going to get a couple pairs of red ones with green stripes.

If they continue to drop the critical score for discharge 1 point a month it will be 37 on February 1 and on February 5th I will have exactly 37. However, according to the paper they may drop it several points the first of the year so, if that is the case, I would be out that much sooner. The days are flying by and I'll be out before you know it. I think I'll make the day I'm discharged as a self-appointed holiday and celebrate it every year.

Those pictures I told you I took are now in the drug store being developed and when I receive them I'll send them to you. Haven't received those 620 films yet, but really appreciate your getting them for me as so far I've been unsuccessful trying to get them here. As I told you in one of my other letters we will be here until the first of the year so you could send me my camera. It shouldn't take more than 8-10 days to arrive. Tell Pete to see if he can pick up some 116 film for it if he can. Maybe Josh could get some for him.

I wish I could be home to spend Thanksgiving and enjoy one of your swell home cooked meals Mother. But maybe I'll make it for Christmas. What day does N.J. celebrate Thanksgiving? We are having our's here on the 22nd and one of the cooks was telling me they are already preparing. They are going to decorate the masthead and have candles on the tables. We all chipped in together in the forward fireroom and bought ourselves a double hotplate. Up at the gallery we manage to get some bread, butter, eggs and sausage and always have something to eat on watch. Boy! you should see the way we make coffee. As yet we haven't a coffee pot so we heat up the water in a gallon can and put the grounds in a clean fuel oil strainer. Some stuff huh? That really keeps you awake on those 12-4 watches.

I heard the broadcast of the Army-Penn game from Franklin Field on Saturday. That was nearly a runaway wasn't it? The announcer said it was a swell day with the temperature in the high 70's. You still must be having some swell weather at home. I suppose you will get all the snow in January and February. Hope you beat that team from North Carolina

Pete. From the looks of those 180 pound guards in the clipping you sent you will have your hands full. You know the old saying–the bigger they come the harder they fall. You won't have to worry about being drafted in March as you can now stay in school and graduate before they take you. By then maybe they will discontinue selective service. Is your class going to Washington or New York?

Hi! there Butz how's the big boy? When are you going to drop me a line? Is your turtle still living? Say Butz, do you think your new Spottie will run me out of the house when I come home? You know he doesn't know me like the old Spottie. Say Mother why didn't you write to the skipper and ask him to let me off a few weeks ago so I could help you house clean? I don't suppose you could get "ole wine bottle" to help you with the the rugs anymore can you as he's pretty old now. You know, the one who lives up on Webster Street? I can't even spell his name. Did you put the storm windows up yet?

Hi! Dad how is the "green atom smasher" holding up? Maybe when I get out and start making some money we can get a new one. I've already seen the 46 Chevrolet's in a show window in Seattle and they're a beauty. Are you still working on a lathe or are you making watch cases? I suppose you will be pretty busy during the Christmas rush. Well folks I must close for now as we are going to general quarters pretty soon.

November 24, 1945
San Diego, Calif.

Dear Folks,

Hello everyone–how is everything back in good ole Riverside? We just came back in last night after operating off the coast for the past few days. I received your letter of the 20th which is fast time from coast to coast. Also received a letter dated September 20th and it must have been lost in the mail as it had a Treasure Island address on it.

Most surprising of all, I received a Christmas package the other day. Nothing unusual about that, except it was from Christmas of 1944. Well, after traveling half way around the globe it finally reached me. That must have been the Valentine package that I received Mother as it had a valentine card in it from you and Dad. It was intact, but one of the containers that had talcum powder in it was busted all over the inside. However, I did manage to salvage a couple packages of razor blades. The gum, candy and magazines were all covered with powder.

We remained in port all day on Thanksgiving and the commissary department really had a swell feed prepared for us. Although I would have much rather been home to spend the day with all of you and watched that football game in the morning. The mess hall was decorated with crepe paper and the tables had white table cloths with a large fruit basket in the center. The baskets had oranges, bananas, apples, grapefruit, nuts, etc. On either side of the fruit baskets were burning candles with 40MM shells for candle sticks. I won't go into detail about the meal as you will be able to read that in the menu I'm sending.

Perhaps you saw in Thursday's paper about the Navy lowering the discharge score again. This is how I stand–On Dec. 26th I will have exactly 36 points. According to the new cut I could have been released on Jan. 1st as then the critical score will be 36. But, as you will see by the clipping, all water tenders and machinist mates are temporarily frozen to 38 points. This is caused by the discharges of WT's and MM's being greater than other rates. The problem is a shortage of water tenders and machinist mates. However, I still think I'll get off the ship after shakedown and possibly get out sometime during the latter part of January or early February. But if they lift the status on my rate I'll get out sooner.

At the present my chances for getting home for either Christmas or New Year's are pretty slim. Of course there's no official dope out yet, but the talk going around is that we are to be back in Seattle on Jan. 6th .

Generally, a ship is never given any leave until after shakedown, but this being the first peacetime Christmas since the war things may be different. If I don't make it at least I know I'll be home for good shortly after and then Christmas of '46 will be surely spent at home. I'll have to make this a short letter folks as I have several clippings to enclose and some pictures. Give my regards to everyone at home and I send my love to all of you.

November 29, 1945
San Diego, Calif.
On Watch

Dear Folks,

At present I'm on watch here in the aft fireroom. It's now 6:30AM, things are running smoothly so now I can take time out to write a few letters. Your two letters, 5 Press's, and the 620 film all arrived this week and I was very glad to receive them. Also, thanks alot for the air mail stamps Mother, but you don't have to send them so often as I can get them out here. By now you should have received my other letter and pictures and I'm also enclosing a few more in this letter which I just got back. It's swell to be able to take pictures of the fellows, views of the ship and scenic views now that the war is over. Alot of the fellows have them now and you see them taking snapshots everywhere. When I get out I can make up a photo album like Dad has from the last war. Also, I have a large 8X10 picture of the Anderson that I'm going to send as soon as I can find a suitable envelope for it. The camera and 116 film haven't arrived as of this date, but I expect them sometime in the middle of the week.

I would have written sooner in the week, but we just returned this afternoon from a six day cruise and didn't have much time to do any writing. As I said before, this shakedown cruise really keeps you "on the go" as we go to G.Q. for firing most of the day from about 8 in the morning till four in the afternoon. We have a shortage of water tenders aboard and we are forced to stand for four hours on and four hours off during the day. I'm putting in my course for WT2/c so that keeps me quite busy too. I hope I'll be able to make it by the 1st of the year.

This morning we had a big job ahead of us. The main steam stop on #2 boiler blew a gasket and we have to replace it. That means holding up the stop with a chain fall where we try to take out about fifteen 8" studs. We'll probably wind up by using a cutting torch to get them off. Had a letter from Hank and he's leaving today to go on leave. Also, it's true about him getting engaged as he said he was giving her a ring for Christmas. I believe she is from Florence although I never met her. The Barton is in San Pedro, Calif. for repairs which is about 150 miles from here. Haven't heard from Bernie, Al, John or Skin in the past few weeks although I dropped them a couple of lines.

Well we finally got hold of a coffee pot so now we can make some good coffee. We have quite a system. Everyone brings something down to the fireroom from the mess hall and we have a midnight snack after the movie at night. The other night we had four loaves of bread, two pounds of butter, two cans of blackberry jam, a gallon of fruit cocktail and about eight pounds of hamburger. Boy! this fireroom looked like a diner during rush hour with all those chow hounds running around.

Your Thanksgiving menu really made my mouth water Mother when I read your letter. That was certainly a feast, I wish I could have been there to enjoy it with you. It was swell to receive the Press's and read up on the hometown news again. By the looks of things the discharge column is growing and the inducted column is getting smaller. I enjoy reading the "sports' and the write up on Riverside's games. The picture of the team was in the Press that arrived yesterday and had a swell write up on Vince. Wish I could have been home to see him play a couple of games.

Well folks I'll have to bring this to a close now as my relief will be coming down soon and I have to write up the log. Give my regards to everyone at home and I send my love to all of you.

December 5, 1945
At Sea

Dear Mother,

We have just secured from General Quarters and so now I can have time to write a few lines. Mother I want you to take my November check and do my Christmas shopping for me as you did last year. I know you will know better than I what Dad, Vince and Butz would like or need and I want you to buy a nice present for yourself. I'd like to buy them and send them myself, but I know I won't have time and as I draw only $19 every two weeks I would have to send for some money anyway. So I hope you will take care of it for me.

In your letter of last week you wanted to know some of my suggestions. Well Mother since I'll be out in a few months I was going to write and tell you not to get anything for me. But if Aunt Elise and Aunt Helen ask I think I'd like all civilian clothes when I get out. Such as shirts 14 ½-15, socks 11 ½, shorts 32, loud ties, a tie pin, of all colors and the loudest ones they can find.

Also Mother as I told you before I want you to take whatever you need from my check when it comes every month. Especially now at Christmas time you will be able to use some extra money and I want you to take it. Boy! Bernie sure got a lucky break in getting transferred, going home on leave and then reporting for his discharge. He had about ¾ points less than me, but his rate isn't frozen. Hank should be home by now. He said that he was coming down to see you when he got home so he may be dropping in soon. Must close now Mother as it's time for chow. Will write more later.

San Diego, Calif.
December 21, 1945
At Sea

Dear Folks,

Hello everyone. I received all your letters and cards this week and was very glad to hear from you. Your Christmas cards were very nice and thanks a million for the $5 Mother and Dad, but you shouldn't have sent it.

Mother yesterday I received your card and letter describing the beautiful winter weather and snow scene. That and having Bing Crosby's "White Christmas" over the radio all this week made me sorta homesick. I've been in the service long enough now to be over ordinary homesickness, but everytime the holidays and Christmas arrive it hits me.

At least I have the consolation of knowing that I will be home very shortly after Christmas. If they hadn't frozen my rate I could have gotten off the ship and discharged by January 1. As it is now my hopes are to get off sometime around February 1. There is alot of talk now that the points are to take a considerable drop on the 1st of the year and drop two points a short while after that. From now on I'm praying and keeping my fingers crossed.

Tell John that I am sure mad at him. He hasn't written to me since I left Treasure Island in October and now he surprises me by getting discharged. Now that he's a civilian he should have lots of time to write. Bernie is sure lucky, if he hadn't 10 points for dependency he'd only be at 26 points and probably wouldn't get out till next year. Had a Christmas card from Skin at Tientsin, China and it took 19 days to arrive. Compared to Skin I am certainly lucky to be in the States at least for the holidays as he has been out there in the islands for 19 months now.

So Earl Hill has also been discharged. Every time I hear about somebody like that it makes my blood boil. I enlisted in the Navy and was on a destroyer convoying about eight months before he was ever in the Army and now he's out before me. That just shows you the comparison between the Army and Navy's point systems. Then every day they come around and "soft soap" you to ship over for another four years. What a laugh.

Well folks they are giving us a leave over Christmas. Yes, a whole few days which wouldn't even cover traveling across country. There are quite a few fellows on the ship who live in California. Alot of us east coasters are standing by for them so they can be home over the holidays. I'm standing by for a water tender from northern California.

Today is our last day of the shakedown cruise. We got underway this morning and are going to drop some depth charges and return to port this afternoon. Then we'll be in over the holidays and leave for the Bremerton, Washington Navy Yard on the 2nd or 3rd and are done there on the 6th of January. There is also some talk about getting a ten day leave while we are in the yard. If so, I'm not even going to take that as it would mean 8 days traveling and 2 days at home besides having to spend alot of money for trains.

It will be only a short time before I'm off the ship for good then I'll have the wonderful feeling of going on a one way trip home and not having to come back again. In your letter that I received on Sunday you said that Hank dropped in to see you. What did you think of his girl? Did he get engaged? When does he report back? I remember him telling me that his time won't be up until next July.

Just got back that roll of film from my camera. It takes swell pictures now that it's been repaired. Those pictures of Butz are swell. Say, the new Spottie does look something like our old one, but not quite as big. How does he like this cold weather? Run right back in the house like our old Spot? When I get out I'm going to try and get a thoroughbred English or Irish setter.

Well folks I must bring this letter to a close now as its 11:30 and about time for chow. I wish all of you a very "Merry Christmas" and want you to know that I'll be thinking of you and wishing I were home to spend it with all of you. Especially to enjoy that swell dinner I know

Mother will have. Give my regards and Christmas wishes to everyone at home for me.

P.S. Say Vince and Butz, throw a few snow balls for me huh? This Calif. sunshine is so warm that a few of the fellows and I had our shirts off yesterday getting a sun tan.

December 30, 1945
San Diego, Calif.

Dear Folks,

By the time you receive this letter I can be wishing all of you "A Happy New Year". This year of 1945 will go down in history with the ending of the war in Europe and the final surrender of Japan.

Yesterday the 29th I received your Christmas package and on the 28th received the fruit cake that Aunt Elise sent. Thanks alot folks as I enjoyed the cookies and candy very much and can use everything that was in the package. The mailroom was really good to me this week as I received about 10-15 letters and Christmas cards. Also I received a very nice brown plaid outdoor shirt from Carolyn. So that gives me a start with my civilian wardrobe already.

How is the weather at home now? Did you have a "White Christmas"? We had a wet one as it rained most of Christmas week, including Christmas Eve. On Christmas Day however, it was a beautiful and warm with a clear blue sky overhead. I had liberty Christmas Eve and a couple of the fellows and I went to midnight Mass in San Diego. I'm enclosing the menu of our Christmas dinner, the Navy only puts out good meals like that on Thanksgiving, 4th of July, Christmas and New Year's. But as I told you before Mother your home cooked meals are like that every day and I'm awaiting the day when I can be home to enjoy them again.

We ended our shakedown cruise on Friday with a battle problem and captain's inspection. At present ½ the crew are on the four day New Year's leave. When they return, which is on the 2nd, we are leaving for the Bremerton, Washington Navy Yard where we will get a 21 day overhaul. We are due to arrive there on the 6th. All hands are supposed to get a 10 day leave while there and, as I told you in one of my other letters, I won't be able to make it home as it would only give me two days at home. The next time I come home it's going to be a one-way trip and I'll be home for good. One of the other water tenders whom I stood by for over Christmas is getting discharged in a few days and he's invited me and another fellow to spend our leave at his place. He lives near Santa Barbara, Calif. and it is very nice country there.

I believe I have some good news for you. After alot of study, work and just plain sweat I've made Watertender Second Class. The assistant engineer's officer told my buddies and I that we both make it Jan 1st. Now I'm assistant in charge of the forward fireroom and have my own steaming watch of five men. Also that will give me a 12 dollar increase in pay each month.

This week I received one of John's "long letters" (?) and he told me about being discharged. Say Mother, next time he comes around you better tap him in the head with a rolling pin as he said there wasn't much doing just now and he was thinking of coming back in the Navy. Now I know that cold weather must have affected him. Yesterday I received a letter from Al, the first I've heard from him in several months. He was in the Admiralty Islands and from there they are going to harbor in the Philippines. I believe his ship is ferrying troops back to the states. Well folks I must sign off for now. Give my regards to everyone at home. With love to all of you.

1946

January 1–Left San Diego for Bremerton.

January 2, 1946
San Diego, Calif.

Dear Folks,

Just a few short lines to let you know that we are leaving this afternoon for Bremerton. We just finished fueling the ship and are supposed to get underway about four o'clock. We are due to arrive on either Saturday or Sunday.

The weather just now, and for the past few days, has been damp and foggy. The radio man told me yesterday that storm warnings are up along the coast so maybe we will run into some rough weather on the way. After being in California for the past two months it will be a cold change going to Washington. They don't have too much snow up there, but it really gets cold at times.

How is everyone at home? I guess Butz and Vince are getting back to school now after the holidays. Had a letter from Skin out in China and he said it was awfully cold there and it snowed a little. He said it was the first he'd seen in 21 months. I imagine it won't be too long before he'll be coming back. It sure would be swell if we two get home at the same time. Well folks it's now ten minutes to two and I have to get this in the mail by two o'clock. So the next time you hear from me I'll be back in Washington. Love to you all.

P.S. Mother, would you send me some more Press's? I'd like to find out how that Army-Navy game came out in Riverside.

January 6—Arrived at Bremerton Navy Yard in Washington state.

January 7, 1946
Bremerton, Washington

Dear Folks,

Hello everyone. I'm now back in this cold state of Washington and brrrrrrr! is it cold. We arrived the afternoon of the 5th after a rather bumpy trip coming up the coast. I suppose I'm just not cut out to be a sailor as the morning of the first day underway I lost my breakfast. Ha! Ha! Almost everyone on my watch was sick, including myself. You should have seen those poor six new firemen. They looked like a green window shade.

Getting back to this climate is quite a sudden change after basking in that Calif. sunshine. It is a clear, brisk cold and rains quite often. I received your very long II section letter of the 28th yesterday and was very glad to hear from you and all the latest news Mother. But did I get mad at you after reading that part where you told me about the Christmas presents. Mother, why didn't you buy a nice dress, pocket-book or something for yourself instead of an umbrella? You know if I would have been home I'd have bought you something much nicer than that. So when I come home I will get you something nice as a Christmas present from me.

Say Pete what's this I hear about you giving a cosmetic set for a present? Who's the lucky girl? I gave Carolyn a spun silver necklace that I bought when I was in Mexico. Did I tell you about the sporty outdoor civilian shirt she sent me? Mother did you receive that package of those things I bought in Mexico? Before we left San Diego I received your Christmas package and Aunt Elise's, but as yet haven't received Aunt Clara's.

Did you ever receive those snapshots I sent some time ago? I don't believe I recall you mentioning in any of your letters that you received them. The camera is in good shape and takes swell pictures since it was fixed. Those pictures you took of Butz and Spot came out nice and I had intended to send them until I dropped some oil on them when I was showing them in the fireroom. So now I'm having a new set made and will send them as soon as they are finished.

Your description of that Christmas dinner you prepared Mother really made my mouth water. I only wish I could have been there to enjoy it with you. But I hope it won't be too long now until I'll be out for good and then I'll be able to enjoy your cooking every day. The first leave section went on their 10 day leave the second we came in here. They return on the 17th and then our ten days start. We changed our mind about going to that fellow's place in Southern California. We are going to Canada instead. I've always wanted to go there and so now I'll have the chance. The border is only 165 miles from here or about a 5 hour ride. I'm going to take my camera along and try to get some good shots of that country. When I go ashore tomorrow I'll have to wire you a telegram for some money as we won't get paid before leave starts and I'll need some money.

Both Bill Ponton and myself made WT2/c and Al Alviso made WT1/c so we had to abide by the Navy tradition and all buy a box of cigars to hand out. Now everytime we go down into the compartment you have to swim through the cigar smoke as everyone's smoking them. As soon as we hit the yard here we secured all four boilers and are now taking steam from the dock. We (the firemen) have to clean firesides on all four and punch tubes. Now on this ship I draw a little more water and so can sit around and drink coffee and let the firemen do the work as I did on the ole Simpson and Barton.

How's your turtles doing Butz? They didn't freeze out in the snow did they? How is Spottie? Hello Dad. Wish I could have been home a few weeks ago to help you with all that painting. I'll bet the rooms look swell now. Are you still busy at the watchcase? The shipyard workers here have cut down to an eight hour 5-days a week. There are hardly any aboard. How is the green beetle running? Is there much of a chance to get a car now as I'd like to try to get a '41-'42 when I get out?

Well, I'll have to close folks as its getting late. Give my regards to everyone back home and say I said "hello". My love to all of you.

January 17-28–Left for Vancouver, B.C. on a 10 day leave.

January 17, 1946
Bremerton, Washington

Dear Folks,

Hello everyone. Sorry I haven't written sooner, but we have been kept pretty busy these past ten days cleaning and putting boilers back together. I received your letter and money order on the 13th which was very fast time. I was lucky that I could send a telegram as the Newark and New York City telegraph offices are on strike. The reason I sent for the money was to use on my ten day leave which starts this afternoon. A couple of my buddies and I are going to Vancouver, B.C. One of the new fellows who just came aboard ship lives there and he is going to try and get a cabin for us. They just came back from the first ten day leave this morning and were telling us about the swell time they had and the beautiful country up there, including the seven feet of snow they just had. So we should have a good time there as I've always wanted to see Canada as long as I can remember.

The weather for the past week has been cold, damp and raining off and on. Sometimes it's sorta half sleet and half snow. When we go over to Seattle we have to go by ferry which is an hour's ride across Puget Sound. It really is beautiful up this time of the year with snow all over the mountains. What kind of weather are you having at home?

We are in dry dock having the bottom scraped and repainted. Our yard availability is supposed to be up on February 5th. Say Pete what's this about you trying to enlist again? I don't blame you for not wanting to get caught in the Army, but can't you wait until you graduate? And also, read any papers you may sign as they enlist you for 2, 4, or 6 years and make sure it's 2. But promise me one thing and that is not to join before I get home which I think will be soon and before your birthday. Well folks I'll have to make this short as they have already announced that leave is starting. Give my regards to everyone and I will drop you a line from Canada. Sending you my love to all.

January 23, 1946
Vancouver, B.C.

Dear Folks,

Hello everyone. Greetings from Canada. I suppose you have been wondering how I am enjoying my stay in the north. Well of all the places I've been I believe this is one of the nicest. It's even better than Seattle. Six of us fellows from the Anderson are staying at the same hotel and we are having a swell time. During the week there are only about 15 or 20 American sailors in town, but alot come in over the weekend. The Canadian people are very friendly and treat us swell.

The weather is even warmer than Seattle, but it is still very cold, clear mountain air. It sometimes rains, but clears up in the evening. Already I am developing a "Canadian appetite" and I mean these people really go in for eating in a big way because the mountain air gives you a big appetite without doing any work.

Nothing is rationed, but they have the meatless days each week on Tuesdays and Fridays. We have been eating in the same restaurant and still haven't repeated on the menu. We've had steaks, ham and mushrooms, chicken, canadian bacon, hot cakes, eggs, etc. The cost of living is much cheaper. Grade A large eggs are 37 cents a dozen and you can buy anything you want in the stores.

The exchange rate on our money is 10 cents on a dollar. So a twenty dollar bill is actually worth $22. The reason I sent for more money is that I am going to try and buy a few civilian things and send them home as they are much cheaper. I sent the telegram on Saturday afternoon and received it on Monday. I've already bought a swell woolen outdoor shirt and sent it home. It's almost as thick as a blanket and I know you couldn't get one like that at home.

Tomorrow we are supposed to see those people about using the cabin in the mountains. You can see them from here towering in the distance. They are covered with snow and large pine, spruce and cedar cover the base. The one we are going to has an elevation of 4600 feet and when the fellows were up there last week it had seven feet of snow piled around the cabin.

The people are very sport conscious and go skiing, hiking, ice skating and have winter sports the year around. Every weekend there is a big ski meet up in the mountains. I brought my camera and several rolls of film with me so I hope to get some swell shots while I'm here.

Our leave isn't up until 8 o'clock on Monday morning so we are going back Sunday night and have reservations on the 6:40 bus. I could go on describing this country all night, but I'm afraid that I couldn't get it all in a letter. So I'll write again when I get back to the ship and tell you all about my trip. Hoping this letter finds all of you in good health. Give my love and regards to everyone at home. Love to you all.

February 2–Ship went out on a full power run.

February 3–1800–Transferred from the ship to a receiving ship on Pier 91 in Seattle.

February 3, 1946
Bremerton, Washington

Dear Folks,

Hello everyone. By this time you must be wondering what's become of me, not having heard from me recently. I'm sorry I didn't write sooner, but ever since returning from my ten day leave we have been busy night and day trying to get the boilers back together. We have just finished up this week and today we went out in Puget Sound for a trial run. Our yard period is supposed to be up on the 8th and then I believe we are to go down to San Diego again to join the rest of the squadron.

This week I received Butz' letter and 4 Press's. It was good to read some of the news from the ole town and see what fellows are home. My, everyone at home seems to be getting married. Helen Dietrich, Kitten Ellis, and I suppose it won't be long before Doris gets married. Have the Hartmans heard from Skin lately? When does he expect to get back? Do you still see much of John? Has he started working yet?

Well folks I suppose you have been wondering how I enjoyed my leave in Canada. I only wish I could describe the beautiful scenery and swell time that I had in this letter. The people in Vancouver really treat the American sailors swell. While we were there we went to visit Bud Flanders' folks. Bud is on the Anderson and lives in Vancouver. His father is a swell fellow. He was in the Canadian Navy for 5 years and has worked in lumber and mining camps. He got the cabin for us, and he, "Red", my buddies and I went into the mountains for the weekend. We went on a Friday night and came down Sunday afternoon as we had to leave that night. The mountain has an elevation of 4600 feet and is five miles from base to summit. That will give you an idea of what climbing we did. Not only that, but we each had a 50 pound napsack full of food that we had to pack up.

When we were about three miles up we began to hit snow and when we finally reached the cabin we had difficulty finding it as it was snowed under. Without a doubt there must have been 8 or 10 feet of snow. That was the most snow I've seen in about eight years. We took about ten dollars worth of "grub" with us and did we eat. Steak, hamburger, sausages, buckwheat cakes, bacon and eggs, soup, hot chocolate etc. That clear mountain air and climate really does wonders for your appetite.

If you really wanted to see something funny you should have seen Red and I take a crack at skiing. Boy! was that a scream and a show in itself. Just wait until you see the pictures we took. I sent three rolls of film and am hoping that they turn out all right. It snowed all day Saturday and Sunday and the trees weighted down with snow looked like a paradise. After those two days of snow we just about were snowed in and had to break our own trail back to the main trail. We would be walking along and all of a sudden find ourselves up over our waist in snow. In all, we spent a wonderful time and the Flanders want Red and I to come back again.

Say Dad how did your party for the fellows turn out? I really had a laugh when Mother told me about the jokes you planned to pull on them. Up to your old tricks again huh? Ha! Ha! Well Pete I guess they can't say you didn't try to get in the Navy after being turned down twice for color blindness. But it will pay you in the long run to graduate. I know you will have a swell time on the Washington trip.

Hi! Butz. How's the scouts coming along? Thanks alot for your letter this week. You really gave me lots of news. Do you think the new Spottie will go after me when I get home? You know he's never seen me. Mother I can't wait until I'm home again for your good cooking. You won't find me the "picky" eater as you used to know as after being in the Navy this long I'll eat anything and like it.

Must bring this to a close now as it's time for lights out. Oh yes, tell Aunt Clara I received her fruit cake this week, but as yet haven't had time to write. Sending my love to you all, I am

Your Sailor Son & Brother
"Fran"

Editor's Note: This was Fran Yearly's last letter from his war years. He was eagerly looking forward to once more becoming a civilian and beginning a new life as a young man. Ironically, exactly thirty years to this day would be his last full day on earth. He died on February 4, 1976.

February 7–My name was on the 155 man train draft to Lido Beach, NY.

February 11–1850–Draft 505–411 men left Seattle for Lido Beach.

Western Union Telegram
Seattle, Washington
February 11, 1946

Mrs. Frank Yearly
300 Lippincott Ave.
Riverside, NJ

HOPE TO SEE YOU SOMETIME NEXT WEEK WITH DISCHARGE. TRAINS HELD UP DUE TO SNOWSTORMS. LOVE FRAN.

February 12–Passed through Washington, Idaho and Montana.

February 13–North Dakota.

Afterword

From a Burlington County, New Jersey newspaper:

D-DAY VETERAN AT HOME

Riverside July 29–Riverside's first boy to arrive home safely from the invasion of France is Francis C. Yearly, Fireman Third Class, son of Mr. and Mrs. Frank Yearly, 300 Lippincott Avenue. He was on a destroyer which bombarded the Normandy beachhead to make way for the invading forces. The ship was struck, but Yearly was not injured.

Yearly enlisted in the Navy in September 1942 and got his training at the Great Lakes Station. Since then he has been stationed in Ireland, England, Scotland, Casablanca and Bermuda.

The Secretary of the Navy
Washington

March 16, 1946

My dear Mr. Yearly:

I have addressed this letter to reach you after all the formalities of your separation from active service are completed. I have done so without formality, but as clearly as I know how to say it. I want the Navy's pride in you, which it is my privilege to express, to reach into your civilian life and to remain with you always.

You have served in the greatest Navy in the world.

It crushed two enemy fleets at once, receiving their surrenders only four months apart. It brought our land-based airpower within bombing range of the enemy and set our ground armies on the beachheads of final victory. It performed the multitude of tasks necessary to support these military operations.

No other Navy at any time has done so much. For your part in these achievements you deserve to be proud as long as you live. The Nation which you served at a time of crisis will remember you with gratitude The best wishes of the Navy go with you into civilian life. Good luck!

Sincerely Yours,
James Forrestal

Written by Scott Whitehouse
USS Barton Medical Officer 12/43 to 10/45

The USS Barton was built at the famous New England shipyard, the Bath Iron Works in Bath, Maine. The keel was laid on May 24, 1943 and the ship was launched on October 10, 1943. The sponsor was Barbara Barton, granddaughter of Rear Admiral John Kennedy Barton, US Navy (1853-1921). Our ship was the second to be named for Admiral Barton, the first was sunk during the Third Battle of Savo Island on the night of November 12-13, 1942.

The Barton was the first 2200-ton class destroyer and given the honor of performing the trials for this class of ships. The trials took place off the coast of Rockland, Maine on December 27-29, 1943. The weather was definitely windy and is well remembered by those "plank owners" who made that memorable trip. The ice froze on the forward gun mounts six inches thick. Looking like an iceberg, the Barton arrived at Boston Navy Yard, Charlestown, where she received a "steam bath" and made ready for the commissioning. The ceremonies took place on the fantail. Commander Joseph Callahan posted the first watch and the Barton began her career.

Due to engine trouble the Barton was late in starting her shakedown cruise. After engine repairs in Norfolk Navy Yard, Portsmouth, Va., the Barton went to Bermuda in March and performed her shakedown training exercises. Everyone enjoyed the quaint colonial atmosphere of Bermuda. All drinks were served with a "finger" of soda mixed in. A little bit of rum really did boil when it got out into the Bermuda sun. Rum made bicycles very difficult to navigate and many men became sea sick in the attempt.

Following the shakedown cruise and minor adjustments in the Boston Navy Yard, the Barton went to Europe in May and began her fighting career by shooting and being shot at by the Nazis. On our way over we helped convoy a group of cargo ships carrying ammunition and tankers carrying aviation gasoline. We arrived without mishap in Greenock, Scotland and steamed down the Irish Sea through the English Channel to Plymouth, England. After seeing how green the Irish Sea is everyone understood why it is named "Irish". Its color is emerald green.

The fog was so thick we were in Plymouth a full day before we could see the town or even make the harbor. Plymouth, with all its bombings, was a sad city to behold. We all agreed that the Pilgrims did a wise thing when they moved from there. On June 3 we left Plymouth and joined the amphibious troops preparing to attack the Normandy Beach. It was a tense night aboard the Barton as we anticipated D-Day and the first combat action of the ship. We were fearful and expectant of the worst. Our assignment the morning of D-Day was to screen the transport area. That afternoon we moved in close to the shore to take the place of a destroyer which had to retire to reammunition the ship.

While here the Barton received a distress signal from a group of Army "Rangers" who were trapped in the niche of a cliff and who had wounded that needed medical attention. It was decided to send the whaleboat after the wounded men. The storming of Normandy by the Barton whaleboat is still a vivid memory. German snipers opened fire on the whaleboat as it neared land. Many of the slugs chewed their way into the gunwales of the boat.

Bacon, PhM2c, was hit by a thirty caliber bullet. The whaleboat returned to the ship without the wounded. Lieutenant Don Kelly, who commanded the expedition, hurried to the bridge to direct the gunfire. The Barton supported the Normandy beach head for three weeks. A German plane was bagged during one of the night raids. All remember the huge ball of fire as the flaming wreck plummeted into the bay. We went with the force sent to bombard the fortress of Cherbourg June 25. Everything seemed peaceful. All hands were sightseeing the Cherbourg coast. The Chief Engineer, Lieutenant Jo Laliberte, saw a flashing light on the shore and made the casual remark, "someone is signaling us". They really were, and they knew where we were, for a few seconds later, "Bang!" and the Barton was hit by German artillery fire. We made a white wake out of there, but FAST. The shell hit the port side of the ship. After temporary patching the Barton returned to the USA via Belfast, Ireland. We arrived in Boston on the second Sunday of July and steamed up the Charles River with our souvenir barrage balloon flying from the fantail. We were the center of gawking attention of the Sunday afternoon excursion boat crowds.

We left Boston bound for the Pacific in September after having repaired the damage we received from the shore batteries of Cherbourg. While on our way to the Panama Canal we received word that a merchant ship had been torpedoed in our vicinity just off Cape Hatteras, North Carolina.We hurried to her rescue and were happy to learn that she could make port without assistance. We hunted for the sub for several days, but had to give up because of a hurricane coming our way. We put into Chesapeake Bay and got out of the main path of the storm.

Leaving there we accompanied the new command ship, USS Eldorado, on her shakedown cruise which was to take her through the Canal up to San Francisco. We separated at San Diego and the Barton spent several days there. Many had the opportunity to visit and obtain mementos of Old Mexico. We arrived at Pearl Harbor in October and spent two weeks there. Everyone satisfied himself about the fabulous Honolulu. Most thought that it was a fairly good place though they would rather be home.

We then proceeded to the south seas. Our first assignment was with the carrier task force which sent air strikes over Manila. Ulithi was the logistics center. After each operation we returned there to reprovision the ship. After several weeks of carrier operation we left Ulithi to join the famous Seventh Fleet in the Philippines. We anchored November 30 in San Pedro Bay, near Taciopar, the provincial capital of Manila. Our first job was to head the Ormoc Landing, the purpose of which was to put troops ashore behind the Jap lines. The site for the landing was also the place where the Japs supported their army with supplies and fresh troops. We arrived in the early dawn of December 7 and the LCI's unloaded their troops without incident or even a casualty. The Barton had a short duel with a shore battery which didn't last long. Some of the shots came uncomfortably near, though.

We started back to San Pedro Bay. That was when we really were introduced to the Japanese Air Force. They started their now famous suicide tactics on us. At that time the fact that the Jap was using a suicide plane and the damage he was producing with it was a closely guarded secret. We were under constant air attack for nine hours. We saw many of our ships hit, burn and sink. One plane dove on us. He was just off our fantail when our gunners scored a hit on the tail of the plane which severed it from the plane and caused it to hedgehop the ship and crash into the sea just in front of the bow. We will never forget our first Jap plane. We later assisted in shooting down another Jap plane. Late in the afternoon a most welcome rainstorm came down and blanketed the whole returning convoy from the view of the Jap Bird-men. After it was over there was general agreement that France had been a pleasure cruise by comparison.

Our next assignment was with the task force making the Mindoro Landing on December 15. While in the neighborhood we sank a Jap freighter. The Mindoro Landing was accomplished without too exciting a time and we returned to San Pedro Bay. Christmas of 1944 was spent in San Pedro Bay. A few got ashore at Talosa where those who could swim did. Others visited with the natives. Christmas was marred by the extensive preparations for the Lingayen Gulf landing. The trip to Lingayen Gulf was without any real incident to the Barton. Once we changed stations a Jap crashed the ship which took our place. We arrived safely at Lingayen Gulf on the night of January 5. The next day we were formally received and went down the kamikaze reception line shaking hands with each Jap on his way to his ancestors. The Walke and the Sumner preceeded us into the Gulf and each was hit by a suicide plane and had to retire. (Editor's note: the Captain and 12 crewmen on the Walke were killed). The Barton, in company with the O'Brien, relieved them. The O'Brien was almost immediately hit and had to retire. About three seconds later a plane got our number and made a straight line dive for us. The plane just did clear the bow and exploded. In fact, it scraped the starboard anchor. Luckily the gasoline didn't explode. Plane fragments and gasoline sprayed the whole ship. That was the first time we had a Jap on board the ship—in part anyway. That night we sank an enemy patrol vessel. We stayed in the Gulf for three days while the minesweeps freed the area of mines.

S Day for the Barton (the day of the Lingayen Gulf Landing was termed S Day), passed without mishap, though several times Japs were close enough for us to get in some shooting. That night several Jap PT boats and suicide swimmers with demolition charges attached to their bodies harassed the Gulf area. We left the Philippines after the Lingayen Operation and arrived at Ulithi Atoll on February 1. Our new assignment was to operate with the carrier task forces. This carrier task force had the ticklish job of carrying out the first mass carrier based bombing of the Japanese homeland.

During the night of the second day of raids the Barton accidentally rammed the USS Ingraham, causing extensive damage to the Barton bow. The Barton and Ingraham left the main task force in company with the Moale and proceeded to Saipan for a complete checkup of our damage. That night three of us sank a three-ship Jap convoy. One of the ships was credited to us though we assisted in the sinking of the other two.

From Saipan we were sent to Guam for the rebuilding of the bow. We left Guam with our new bow and proceeded to Ulithi where we made all the preparations for the Okinawa campaign. We arrived at Okinawa on L minus 5. The day after we arrived a suicide plane missed us by a bare one hundred feet. A few minutes later we assisted in shooting down another plane. One of those I'll never forget occurred when the Barton was assigned to patrol off the shore. It was our duty to harass the enemy. Maybe we were harassed more than the Japs. Anyway we were patrolling off one of the main Jap airfields, Yontan, in the central part of the island. The patrol was of such a nature that we were the only ship of any size there. We had numerous air raids and had been to general quarters several times during the night. We had observed several Jap planes landing on the airfield with their landing lights glowing. All of a sudden with no advance warning a Jap seaplane swooped out of the night sky and just barely missed our bridge. To those who saw the plane directly above the ship a prickly sensation still accompanies the thought.

The landing on the beach head of Okinawa was without incident to the Barton. No one will ever forget the din, the steady cackle of 40 millimeter machine gun fire, the coughing swoosh of the rockets and concussion of our five inch artillery fire. Our primary mission at Okinawa was fire support for the Army and Marines. We fired night and day for over three months. All our five inch mounts were completely worn out by the firing of over 22,000 rounds. Insofar as we were able to determine, the Barton fired more large caliber artillery projectiles at the island of Okinawa than any other destroyer ever fired at any one engagement in the history of naval warfare. We were constantly loading and firing. Loading and firing. This kept up day after day, night after night, yet through it all the Barton crew withstood the physical torture and mental strain in the most admirable way. The upkeep of the ship was left to the elements. The Barton became the Old Barton during the operation. Stanchions fell. Bulkheads rusted. Fiber glass insulation fell. Many of the boys still carry fiber glass insulation in their skin.

To the Barton belongs the distinct honor of firing the last naval artillery fire at the Jap installations before the final mop up of the Japs on Okinawa. The island was declared to be secured on June 22. Our next job was to go with the minesweeping group which was sweeping mines from the East China Sea. Here we sank many of the mines swept up by the minesweeps. There was no enemy action that stirred us. We left Okinawa in the middle of July and proceeded to Leyte, Philippines Islands for a much needed overhaul and rest. While on the way we discovered the sinking Underhill, a destroyer which had been torpedoed and left sinking by a Jap sub. We were unable to recover any live personnel. We searched for the sub with unfruitful results.

At Leyte everyone had a good time. The natives were bargained with for various articles. The favorite was to buy a bolo knife. It was while we were in Leyte that the Japs hollered "uncle" and offered to surrender. It was with yelling, shooting of rockets and playing the sky with our searchlight that we celebrated the news. On August 14 we received the mission of carrying the New Zealand government representative to the Battleship Missouri for the Jap surrender ceremonies. It was with interest that we viewed the warm greeting that he received from Admiral Halsey as he was placed on the deck of the battleship via a pulley chair swung on a line between the Barton and the Missouri. We operated with the covering carrier task force during the surrender ceremonies and for three weeks after. We then steamed into Tokyo Bay–mission accomplished. Destination Tokyo–arrived.

Everyone had the opportunity to go ashore and view at first hand the "little monkey men" of Japan. We agreed that the name of "little monkey men" was an apt one. We marveled at his ability to wage war with so little for so long. To those who had to be content with the high prices of second hand Jap souvenirs at the Jap battlefronts it was great fun to be able to collect at first hand all they had any desire for. Many got rifles, shotguns, china, tools, dolls, fans, kimonos and obis. The Barton left Tokyo Bay and went to Okinawa where she picked up returning members of the armed forces and proceeded home via the Great Circle Route arriving in Seattle on October 19, 1945.

The Barton had fought on two battle fronts and steamed a total of 86,164 miles. Her record to this date may have been bettered by some, but her satisfaction at having done her part cannot be bettered. Above all everyone rejoiced that the war was over and that the Barton, the Sleezy B, the Lucky B, fought her share well and had returned home without loss of life or limb to any member of the Barton crew in spite of all the narrow escapes.

23 November 1944

CAPTAIN'S MEMORANDUM TO THE CREW:

This ship is entering and will continue to operate in enemy infested areas, during which enemy planes, subs, PT boats and other naval surface craft may be encountered at any time.

The safety of this ship and the lives of those on board will depend upon:

Promptly manning battle stations at general quarters or whenever ordered. Effectively and to the utmost of each man's ability, performing his assigned duties with skill, intelligence, determination, alertness, calm thinking and efficiency for each minute of every hour while at general quarters or condition watches.

General quarters will be ordered on the *alarm* when the enemy is discovered or reported in the vicinity. Periods at battle stations may be sometimes long and tiresome–we must be prepared to hit the enemy first. Do not relax from alertness and ability to fight even though you may be tired from lack of sleep–the enemy is just as tired, but if he catches us unprepared, he has the advantage.

Flash Burns from bombs and shellfire have killed many men in the past on boad our ships because they were not adequately clothed. To protect your own life, all hands <u>will</u> now and while in combat areas at all times, except when turned in, wear a complete uniform covering the entire body except for hands and face. This means shirt with sleeves rolled down, full length trousers, socks, shoes and hat. In addition to the above, all hands will wear lifebelts except that those in exposed weather deck stations will, if nature of duties permit, wear a KAPOK life jacket to protect them from shell and bomb splinters and fragments. All men having exposed battle stations, such as automatic weapons, torpedo, lookout and signal personnel will also be provided with flash protective face mask and gloves which will be worn when enemy attacks are imminent.

During the coming months this ship will probably see much action against the enemy. There will be long hours, many hardships and little rest for any of us. The Captain well appreciates these difficulties and will do all possible to ease these hardships. However, our Country and your folks at home expect us to lick these damned Japs at every turn and finish this war. After that we can return and take a deserved rest. Meanwhile it will take all we've got in the way of smart fighting and alert attention to the big task of winning every fight. The Captain has confidence that the crew of the BARTON can do it if every man does his duty to the fullest extent of his abilities.

E.B. Dexter

From: Engineering Officer
To: All Engineering Personnel

It gives me great pleasure to bring to your attention subject letter written to me by Captain Dexter upon being detached.

18 May 1945

From: The Commanding Officer
To: Lieutenant Joseph H. Laliberte, US Navy, Engineer Officer, U.S.S. BARTON (DD7722).
Subject: Outstanding Performance of the Engineering Department

Upon completion of my assignment as commanding officer and since I may not have an opportunity to personally compliment the members of your department I wish you could convey to every officer and enlisted man in your department my sincere appreciation for the outstanding performance of the entire Engineer Department during the period of my command.

The prolonged, hazardous and extremely strenuous battle operating conditions of the past six months imposed a severe test and challenge to the entire ship's company. Much of the glory for knocking down enemy planes and in general "slapping the Japs around" naturally goes to those who fire the guns. However, it is my opinion that every engineer at his vitally important station below the water line is an unseen, but not unsung here. It is not easy to fulfill one's job in confined spaces below decks where high pressure steam lines are ever a constant source of danger under attack.

For professional skill, "guts" and splendid achievement there is no better crew in any ship and in any ocean than the Barton's and the engineer gang has contributed a great part toward the fine record of the Barton "cannon-ball".

A "WELL DONE", the best of luck, my admiration and hopes of again being shipmates with many BARTON engineers.

E.B. Dexter

From the Barton ship's news letter:

JUNE 1944
DISPATCH RECEIVED FROM DTF 129

1. Though badly handicapped by poor spotting conditions ashore and seriously threatened by efficient enemy batteries you gave a fine performance of greatest value to the army at a crucial time. The Destroyers were particularly resourceful and bold. All ships did their full duty. WELL DONE.......

2. There is a shortage of bowls and cups in the mess hall caused by men taking them out to finish meals elsewhere and to use with privately owned coffee pots. This practice will cease immediately and P.O.'s will put on the report anyone observed removing mess hall gear from the mess hall.

E.G. Sanderson
Lt. Cmdr. US Navy
Executive Officer

From the Barton ship's news letter:

News from Hollywood:
20 Nov '44
The Cavalcade of America this evening presented a radio program featuring movie screen star Robert Montgomery. He spoke on the D-Day invasion of Normandy and his experiences and "what a fine bunch of American boys he had with him through the battles" aboard the U.S.S. Barton.

From the Barton's Ship's news letter:

U.S.S. Barton

7 September 1945
A year has passed since we left Boston and–now that the war is over–I can tell you a great deal about what I have done. Of course, there are some things which still cannot be written, but I am saving those until I see you.

The first incident of an eventful year occurred soon after we left Boston. We received word that a merchant ship had been torpedoed. We hurried to her rescue and were happy to learn she could make port under her own power. We commenced searching for the submarine, but were forced to break off the search and put in to Norfolk to escape a hurricane.

As soon as the weather calmed we resumed our travels. The passage through the Panama Canal was the high spot of the trip. We spent a few days at San Diego and many of the men went to Mexico.

We left the States on October 2, proceeded to Pearl Harbor and arrived there on October 9. All of us enjoyed our trips to the Waikiki Beach. The curfew limited our activities, but we all tried to have our fun as we knew that it would be our last time in civilization for a long while–and what a long while it has been !!!

We left Pearl in company with our entire squadron: Barton, Walke, Laffey, O'Brien, Sumner, Moale, Ingraham and Cooper. I can tell you now that the Barton is the only one of those ships that has remained out here ever since. The Cooper was sunk in December, and the others all went back to the states at various times to undergo repairs–all of which were battle damage. All of us were proud of our ship and the record she has made.

When we arrived at Ulithi we reported for duty with the famed Task Force 38. We participated in air strikes on Yap, Manila and Northern Luzon. We then transferred to the Seventh Fleet and went in on the Ormoc Bay Landing. The landing itself was not difficult, our only action was shore bombardment and a brief duel with a shore battery. On our way to Leyte, however, we had a harrowing introduction to Japanese air attacks. We were under attack for nine hours and saw many of our ships hit. One plane dove on us and missed by 75 feet. That was our first introduction to the Kamikaze Kids–and let me tell you it scared me but *plenty.* We assisted in shooting down another plane. When it was over there was general agreement that France had been a pleasure cruise in comparison.

Our next engagement was the Mindoro Landing. It was comparatively easy, we sank our first enemy ship, a freighter. The next assignment was at Lingayen Gulf. The Kamikaze Kids were working overtime to welcome us. Two of the ships from our squadron entered the Gulf and both were hit by suicide planes. The Barton and another sister ship relieved them and our companion was hit by a plane almost immediately. About three seconds later a Jap selected us for his target and started diving. This was our second experience with the "Divine Wind" and it was our closest call. The plane missed us by inches and we were showered with gasoline and fragments of the plane. There was enough metal on board to give each of us a souvenir.

After the destroyer retired we were left alone in the Gulf to protect the minesweeps. We spent the next few hours wondering which would get us first: a plane or a mine. Another plane made a try, but we shot him down 100 yards away. Late that afternoon we were joined by another destroyer and the two of us collaborated in sinking an enemy patrol craft that night. We stayed there in the Gulf for two more days until the minesweeping was completed. We added an assist on a plane to our record. We returned to Ulithi for routine maintenance and rest. That "rest" part is somewhat ambiguous; sometimes I think we work harder in port then we do at sea. We do, however, have a chance to go on liberty and drink a few beers.

Our next duty was the first carrier air strike on Tokyo. This operation was in support of the landings of Iwo Jima. We expected an all out reaction by the Japs, but we didn't see a single enemy plane. While returning to Guam, with two other destroyers, the three of us combined to sink three Japs ships, credit for one was assigned to us. After leaving Guam we proceeded to Okinawa with the first group of ships. The day after we arrived a suicide plane missed us by a matter of a few yards. A few minutes later we assisted in shooting down another plane. That was what might be called a "warm welcome". Two days later we brought down two planes and assisted on a third. The following day we attacked a sub and got it. All of this action occurred before our troops landed. Later we splashed one plane and assisted on a second.

Our primary mission at Okinawa was fire support for the Army and Marines and we fired day and night for three months. The only rest we had was loading ammunition–and that isn't exactly rest. I didn't get ashore for three months. We fired over 22,000 rounds at Okinawa we believe that is more than any ship has ever fired in a single operation. The Barton has been recommended for a high award for its outstanding performance in that campaign. After the Island was secured we remained in the vicinity for another month as a covering force. That explains why you didn't see the Barton mentioned as one of the ships bombarding Japan. Finally we returned to Leyte for a needed overhaul.

We were at Leyte when the news was received that the Japs had agreed to surrender. That was one happy moment. We left Leyte August 14 and made tracks for a rendezvous with the Third Fleet which was blockading the Japanese main islands. That brings us up to date as that is where we have been ever since. This might almost be called a happy ending–but the states still beckon to us from afar. Arrival in the states will be a happy ending to a long drawn out war.

Notes

Front Cover: November 1942. Home on leave from boot camp.
Back Cover: March 1946. Back home for good.

About the Author

Francis Carl Yearly was born on March 28, 1925, the first of three sons to Louise and Frank Yearly. "Fran" spent his childhood in Riverside, New Jersey, a small town that sits along the Delaware River. He graduated from Riverside High School in June 1942, a few months past his 17th birthday. He enlisted in the Navy in October of that year. For the next three and a half years he served on destroyers that participated in some of the most important sea and land battles of World War II.

Fran received an honorable discharge in February of 1946. He married Mary Wilson on June 19, 1951 and had two daughters and a son. In 1960 they moved to Audubon, New Jersey where they lived until Fran's death from cancer on February 4, 1976. He is buried in St. Mary's Cemetery in Bellmawr, New Jersey.